C-1345 CAREER EXAMINATION SERIES

This is your
PASSBOOK for...

Library Assistant

Test Preparation Study Guide
Questions & Answers

COPYRIGHT NOTICE

This book is SOLELY intended for, is sold ONLY to, and its use is RESTRICTED to individual, bona fide applicants or candidates who qualify by virtue of having seriously filed applications for appropriate license, certificate, professional and/or promotional advancement, higher school matriculation, scholarship, or other legitimate requirements of education and/or governmental authorities.

This book is NOT intended for use, class instruction, tutoring, training, duplication, copying, reprinting, excerption, or adaptation, etc., by:

1) Other publishers
2) Proprietors and/or Instructors of "Coaching" and/or Preparatory Courses
3) Personnel and/or Training Divisions of commercial, industrial, and governmental organizations
4) Schools, colleges, or universities and/or their departments and staffs, including teachers and other personnel
5) Testing Agencies or Bureaus
6) Study groups which seek by the purchase of a single volume to copy and/or duplicate and/or adapt this material for use by the group as a whole without having purchased individual volumes for each of the members of the group
7) Et al.

Such persons would be in violation of appropriate Federal and State statutes.

PROVISION OF LICENSING AGREEMENTS – Recognized educational, commercial, industrial, and governmental institutions and organizations, and others legitimately engaged in educational pursuits, including training, testing, and measurement activities, may address request for a licensing agreement to the copyright owners, who will determine whether, and under what conditions, including fees and charges, the materials in this book may be used them. In other words, a licensing facility exists for the legitimate use of the material in this book on other than an individual basis. However, it is asseverated and affirmed here that the material in this book CANNOT be used without the receipt of the express permission of such a licensing agreement from the Publishers. Inquiries re licensing should be addressed to the company, attention rights and permissions department.

All rights reserved, including the right of reproduction in whole or in part, in any form or by any means, electronic or mechanical, including photocopying, recording, or by any information storage and retrieval system, without permission in writing from the Publisher.

Copyright © 2024 by
National Learning Corporation

212 Michael Drive, Syosset, NY 11791
(516) 921-8888 • www.passbooks.com
E-mail: info@passbooks.com

PUBLISHED IN THE UNITED STATES OF AMERICA

PASSBOOK® SERIES

THE *PASSBOOK® SERIES* has been created to prepare applicants and candidates for the ultimate academic battlefield – the examination room.

At some time in our lives, each and every one of us may be required to take an examination – for validation, matriculation, admission, qualification, registration, certification, or licensure.

Based on the assumption that every applicant or candidate has met the basic formal educational standards, has taken the required number of courses, and read the necessary texts, the *PASSBOOK® SERIES* furnishes the one special preparation which may assure passing with confidence, instead of failing with insecurity. Examination questions – together with answers – are furnished as the basic vehicle for study so that the mysteries of the examination and its compounding difficulties may be eliminated or diminished by a sure method.

This book is meant to help you pass your examination provided that you qualify and are serious in your objective.

The entire field is reviewed through the huge store of content information which is succinctly presented through a provocative and challenging approach – the question-and-answer method.

A climate of success is established by furnishing the correct answers at the end of each test.

You soon learn to recognize types of questions, forms of questions, and patterns of questioning. You may even begin to anticipate expected outcomes.

You perceive that many questions are repeated or adapted so that you can gain acute insights, which may enable you to score many sure points.

You learn how to confront new questions, or types of questions, and to attack them confidently and work out the correct answers.

You note objectives and emphases, and recognize pitfalls and dangers, so that you may make positive educational adjustments.

Moreover, you are kept fully informed in relation to new concepts, methods, practices, and directions in the field.

You discover that you are actually taking the examination all the time: you are preparing for the examination by "taking" an examination, not by reading extraneous and/or supererogatory textbooks.

In short, this PASSBOOK®, used directedly, should be an important factor in helping you to pass your test.

LIBRARY ASSISTANT

DUTIES
An employee in this class performs paraprofessional library work under the direct supervision of a professional staff member. Although some latitude for independent judgment may be permitted after training has been completed, supervision continues to be exercised by a professional supervisor. Does related work as required.

SCOPE OF THE EXAMINATION
The written test will cover knowledge, skills, and/or abilities in such areas as:
1. Library terminology and practices;
2. Preparing written material;
3. Understanding and interpreting written material;
4. Understanding and interpreting tabular material; and
5. Basic computer usage.

HOW TO TAKE A TEST

I. YOU MUST PASS AN EXAMINATION

A. *WHAT EVERY CANDIDATE SHOULD KNOW*

Examination applicants often ask us for help in preparing for the written test. What can I study in advance? What kinds of questions will be asked? How will the test be given? How will the papers be graded?

As an applicant for a civil service examination, you may be wondering about some of these things. Our purpose here is to suggest effective methods of advance study and to describe civil service examinations.

Your chances for success on this examination can be increased if you know how to prepare. Those "pre-examination jitters" can be reduced if you know what to expect. You can even experience an adventure in good citizenship if you know why civil service exams are given.

B. *WHY ARE CIVIL SERVICE EXAMINATIONS GIVEN?*

Civil service examinations are important to you in two ways. As a citizen, you want public jobs filled by employees who know how to do their work. As a job seeker, you want a fair chance to compete for that job on an equal footing with other candidates. The best-known means of accomplishing this two-fold goal is the competitive examination.

Exams are widely publicized throughout the nation. They may be administered for jobs in federal, state, city, municipal, town or village governments or agencies.

Any citizen may apply, with some limitations, such as the age or residence of applicants. Your experience and education may be reviewed to see whether you meet the requirements for the particular examination. When these requirements exist, they are reasonable and applied consistently to all applicants. Thus, a competitive examination may cause you some uneasiness now, but it is your privilege and safeguard.

C. *HOW ARE CIVIL SERVICE EXAMS DEVELOPED?*

Examinations are carefully written by trained technicians who are specialists in the field known as "psychological measurement," in consultation with recognized authorities in the field of work that the test will cover. These experts recommend the subject matter areas or skills to be tested; only those knowledges or skills important to your success on the job are included. The most reliable books and source materials available are used as references. Together, the experts and technicians judge the difficulty level of the questions.

Test technicians know how to phrase questions so that the problem is clearly stated. Their ethics do not permit "trick" or "catch" questions. Questions may have been tried out on sample groups, or subjected to statistical analysis, to determine their usefulness.

Written tests are often used in combination with performance tests, ratings of training and experience, and oral interviews. All of these measures combine to form the best-known means of finding the right person for the right job.

II. HOW TO PASS THE WRITTEN TEST

A. NATURE OF THE EXAMINATION

To prepare intelligently for civil service examinations, you should know how they differ from school examinations you have taken. In school you were assigned certain definite pages to read or subjects to cover. The examination questions were quite detailed and usually emphasized memory. Civil service exams, on the other hand, try to discover your present ability to perform the duties of a position, plus your potentiality to learn these duties. In other words, a civil service exam attempts to predict how successful you will be. Questions cover such a broad area that they cannot be as minute and detailed as school exam questions.

In the public service similar kinds of work, or positions, are grouped together in one "class." This process is known as *position-classification*. All the positions in a class are paid according to the salary range for that class. One class title covers all of these positions, and they are all tested by the same examination.

B. FOUR BASIC STEPS

1) Study the announcement

How, then, can you know what subjects to study? Our best answer is: "Learn as much as possible about the class of positions for which you've applied." The exam will test the knowledge, skills and abilities needed to do the work.

Your most valuable source of information about the position you want is the official exam announcement. This announcement lists the training and experience qualifications. Check these standards and apply only if you come reasonably close to meeting them.

The brief description of the position in the examination announcement offers some clues to the subjects which will be tested. Think about the job itself. Review the duties in your mind. Can you perform them, or are there some in which you are rusty? Fill in the blank spots in your preparation.

Many jurisdictions preview the written test in the exam announcement by including a section called "Knowledge and Abilities Required," "Scope of the Examination," or some similar heading. Here you will find out specifically what fields will be tested.

2) Review your own background

Once you learn in general what the position is all about, and what you need to know to do the work, ask yourself which subjects you already know fairly well and which need improvement. You may wonder whether to concentrate on improving your strong areas or on building some background in your fields of weakness. When the announcement has specified "some knowledge" or "considerable knowledge," or has used adjectives like "beginning principles of…" or "advanced … methods," you can get a clue as to the number and difficulty of questions to be asked in any given field. More questions, and hence broader coverage, would be included for those subjects which are more important in the work. Now weigh your strengths and weaknesses against the job requirements and prepare accordingly.

3) Determine the level of the position

Another way to tell how intensively you should prepare is to understand the level of the job for which you are applying. Is it the entering level? In other words, is this the position in which beginners in a field of work are hired? Or is it an intermediate or advanced level? Sometimes this is indicated by such words as "Junior" or "Senior" in the class title. Other jurisdictions use Roman numerals to designate the level – Clerk I, Clerk II, for example. The word "Supervisor" sometimes appears in the title. If the level is not indicated by the title, check the description of duties. Will you be working under very close supervision, or will you have responsibility for independent decisions in this work?

4) Choose appropriate study materials

Now that you know the subjects to be examined and the relative amount of each subject to be covered, you can choose suitable study materials. For beginning level jobs, or even advanced ones, if you have a pronounced weakness in some aspect of your training, read a modern, standard textbook in that field. Be sure it is up to date and has general coverage. Such books are normally available at your library, and the librarian will be glad to help you locate one. For entry-level positions, questions of appropriate difficulty are chosen -- neither highly advanced questions, nor those too simple. Such questions require careful thought but not advanced training.

If the position for which you are applying is technical or advanced, you will read more advanced, specialized material. If you are already familiar with the basic principles of your field, elementary textbooks would waste your time. Concentrate on advanced textbooks and technical periodicals. Think through the concepts and review difficult problems in your field.

These are all general sources. You can get more ideas on your own initiative, following these leads. For example, training manuals and publications of the government agency which employs workers in your field can be useful, particularly for technical and professional positions. A letter or visit to the government department involved may result in more specific study suggestions, and certainly will provide you with a more definite idea of the exact nature of the position you are seeking.

III. KINDS OF TESTS

Tests are used for purposes other than measuring knowledge and ability to perform specified duties. For some positions, it is equally important to test ability to make adjustments to new situations or to profit from training. In others, basic mental abilities not dependent on information are essential. Questions which test these things may not appear as pertinent to the duties of the position as those which test for knowledge and information. Yet they are often highly important parts of a fair examination. For very general questions, it is almost impossible to help you direct your study efforts. What we can do is to point out some of the more common of these general abilities needed in public service positions and describe some typical questions.

1) General information

Broad, general information has been found useful for predicting job success in some kinds of work. This is tested in a variety of ways, from vocabulary lists to questions about current events. Basic background in some field of work, such as sociology or economics, may be sampled in a group of questions. Often these are principles which have become familiar to most persons through exposure rather than through formal training. It is difficult to advise you how to study for these questions; being alert to the world around you is our best suggestion.

2) Verbal ability

An example of an ability needed in many positions is verbal or language ability. Verbal ability is, in brief, the ability to use and understand words. Vocabulary and grammar tests are typical measures of this ability. Reading comprehension or paragraph interpretation questions are common in many kinds of civil service tests. You are given a paragraph of written material and asked to find its central meaning.

3) Numerical ability

Number skills can be tested by the familiar arithmetic problem, by checking paired lists of numbers to see which are alike and which are different, or by interpreting charts and graphs. In the latter test, a graph may be printed in the test booklet which you are asked to use as the basis for answering questions.

4) Observation

A popular test for law-enforcement positions is the observation test. A picture is shown to you for several minutes, then taken away. Questions about the picture test your ability to observe both details and larger elements.

5) Following directions

In many positions in the public service, the employee must be able to carry out written instructions dependably and accurately. You may be given a chart with several columns, each column listing a variety of information. The questions require you to carry out directions involving the information given in the chart.

6) Skills and aptitudes

Performance tests effectively measure some manual skills and aptitudes. When the skill is one in which you are trained, such as typing or shorthand, you can practice. These tests are often very much like those given in business school or high school courses. For many of the other skills and aptitudes, however, no short-time preparation can be made. Skills and abilities natural to you or that you have developed throughout your lifetime are being tested.

Many of the general questions just described provide all the data needed to answer the questions and ask you to use your reasoning ability to find the answers. Your best preparation for these tests, as well as for tests of facts and ideas, is to be at your physical and mental best. You, no doubt, have your own methods of getting into an exam-taking mood and keeping "in shape." The next section lists some ideas on this subject.

IV. KINDS OF QUESTIONS

Only rarely is the "essay" question, which you answer in narrative form, used in civil service tests. Civil service tests are usually of the short-answer type. Full instructions for answering these questions will be given to you at the examination. But in case this is your first experience with short-answer questions and separate answer sheets, here is what you need to know:

1) Multiple-choice Questions

Most popular of the short-answer questions is the "multiple choice" or "best answer" question. It can be used, for example, to test for factual knowledge, ability to solve problems or judgment in meeting situations found at work.

A multiple-choice question is normally one of three types—
- It can begin with an incomplete statement followed by several possible endings. You are to find the one ending which *best* completes the statement, although some of the others may not be entirely wrong.
- It can also be a complete statement in the form of a question which is answered by choosing one of the statements listed.

- It can be in the form of a problem – again you select the best answer.

Here is an example of a multiple-choice question with a discussion which should give you some clues as to the method for choosing the right answer:

When an employee has a complaint about his assignment, the action which will *best* help him overcome his difficulty is to
    A. discuss his difficulty with his coworkers
    B. take the problem to the head of the organization
    C. take the problem to the person who gave him the assignment
    D. say nothing to anyone about his complaint

In answering this question, you should study each of the choices to find which is best. Consider choice "A" – Certainly an employee may discuss his complaint with fellow employees, but no change or improvement can result, and the complaint remains unresolved. Choice "B" is a poor choice since the head of the organization probably does not know what assignment you have been given, and taking your problem to him is known as "going over the head" of the supervisor. The supervisor, or person who made the assignment, is the person who can clarify it or correct any injustice. Choice "C" is, therefore, correct. To say nothing, as in choice "D," is unwise. Supervisors have and interest in knowing the problems employees are facing, and the employee is seeking a solution to his problem.

2) True/False Questions

The "true/false" or "right/wrong" form of question is sometimes used. Here a complete statement is given. Your job is to decide whether the statement is right or wrong.

SAMPLE: A roaming cell-phone call to a nearby city costs less than a non-roaming call to a distant city.

This statement is wrong, or false, since roaming calls are more expensive.
This is not a complete list of all possible question forms, although most of the others are variations of these common types. You will always get complete directions for answering questions. Be sure you understand *how* to mark your answers – ask questions until you do.

V. RECORDING YOUR ANSWERS

Computer terminals are used more and more today for many different kinds of exams.
For an examination with very few applicants, you may be told to record your answers in the test booklet itself. Separate answer sheets are much more common. If this separate answer sheet is to be scored by machine – and this is often the case – it is highly important that you mark your answers correctly in order to get credit.
An electronic scoring machine is often used in civil service offices because of the speed with which papers can be scored. Machine-scored answer sheets must be marked with a pencil, which will be given to you. This pencil has a high graphite content which responds to the electronic scoring machine. As a matter of fact, stray dots may register as answers, so do not let your pencil rest on the answer sheet while you are pondering the correct answer. Also, if your pencil lead breaks or is otherwise defective, ask for another.

Since the answer sheet will be dropped in a slot in the scoring machine, be careful not to bend the corners or get the paper crumpled.

The answer sheet normally has five vertical columns of numbers, with 30 numbers to a column. These numbers correspond to the question numbers in your test booklet. After each number, going across the page are four or five pairs of dotted lines. These short dotted lines have small letters or numbers above them. The first two pairs may also have a "T" or "F" above the letters. This indicates that the first two pairs only are to be used if the questions are of the true-false type. If the questions are multiple choice, disregard the "T" and "F" and pay attention only to the small letters or numbers.

Answer your questions in the manner of the sample that follows:

32. The largest city in the United States is
    A. Washington, D.C.
    B. New York City
    C. Chicago
    D. Detroit
    E. San Francisco

1) Choose the answer you think is best. (New York City is the largest, so "B" is correct.)
2) Find the row of dotted lines numbered the same as the question you are answering. (Find row number 32)
3) Find the pair of dotted lines corresponding to the answer. (Find the pair of lines under the mark "B.")
4) Make a solid black mark between the dotted lines.

VI. BEFORE THE TEST

Common sense will help you find procedures to follow to get ready for an examination. Too many of us, however, overlook these sensible measures. Indeed, nervousness and fatigue have been found to be the most serious reasons why applicants fail to do their best on civil service tests. Here is a list of reminders:

- Begin your preparation early – Don't wait until the last minute to go scurrying around for books and materials or to find out what the position is all about.
- Prepare continuously – An hour a night for a week is better than an all-night cram session. This has been definitely established. What is more, a night a week for a month will return better dividends than crowding your study into a shorter period of time.
- Locate the place of the exam – You have been sent a notice telling you when and where to report for the examination. If the location is in a different town or otherwise unfamiliar to you, it would be well to inquire the best route and learn something about the building.
- Relax the night before the test – Allow your mind to rest. Do not study at all that night. Plan some mild recreation or diversion; then go to bed early and get a good night's sleep.
- Get up early enough to make a leisurely trip to the place for the test – This way unforeseen events, traffic snarls, unfamiliar buildings, etc. will not upset you.
- Dress comfortably – A written test is not a fashion show. You will be known by number and not by name, so wear something comfortable.

- Leave excess paraphernalia at home – Shopping bags and odd bundles will get in your way. You need bring only the items mentioned in the official notice you received; usually everything you need is provided. Do not bring reference books to the exam. They will only confuse those last minutes and be taken away from you when in the test room.
- Arrive somewhat ahead of time – If because of transportation schedules you must get there very early, bring a newspaper or magazine to take your mind off yourself while waiting.
- Locate the examination room – When you have found the proper room, you will be directed to the seat or part of the room where you will sit. Sometimes you are given a sheet of instructions to read while you are waiting. Do not fill out any forms until you are told to do so; just read them and be prepared.
- Relax and prepare to listen to the instructions
- If you have any physical problem that may keep you from doing your best, be sure to tell the test administrator. If you are sick or in poor health, you really cannot do your best on the exam. You can come back and take the test some other time.

VII. AT THE TEST

The day of the test is here and you have the test booklet in your hand. The temptation to get going is very strong. Caution! There is more to success than knowing the right answers. You must know how to identify your papers and understand variations in the type of short-answer question used in this particular examination. Follow these suggestions for maximum results from your efforts:

1) Cooperate with the monitor

The test administrator has a duty to create a situation in which you can be as much at ease as possible. He will give instructions, tell you when to begin, check to see that you are marking your answer sheet correctly, and so on. He is not there to guard you, although he will see that your competitors do not take unfair advantage. He wants to help you do your best.

2) Listen to all instructions

Don't jump the gun! Wait until you understand all directions. In most civil service tests you get more time than you need to answer the questions. So don't be in a hurry. Read each word of instructions until you clearly understand the meaning. Study the examples, listen to all announcements and follow directions. Ask questions if you do not understand what to do.

3) Identify your papers

Civil service exams are usually identified by number only. You will be assigned a number; you must not put your name on your test papers. Be sure to copy your number correctly. Since more than one exam may be given, copy your exact examination title.

4) Plan your time

Unless you are told that a test is a "speed" or "rate of work" test, speed itself is usually not important. Time enough to answer all the questions will be provided, but this does not mean that you have all day. An overall time limit has been set. Divide the total time (in minutes) by the number of questions to determine the approximate time you have for each question.

5) **Do not linger over difficult questions**

If you come across a difficult question, mark it with a paper clip (useful to have along) and come back to it when you have been through the booklet. One caution if you do this – be sure to skip a number on your answer sheet as well. Check often to be sure that you have not lost your place and that you are marking in the row numbered the same as the question you are answering.

6) **Read the questions**

Be sure you know what the question asks! Many capable people are unsuccessful because they failed to *read* the questions correctly.

7) **Answer all questions**

Unless you have been instructed that a penalty will be deducted for incorrect answers, it is better to guess than to omit a question.

8) **Speed tests**

It is often better NOT to guess on speed tests. It has been found that on timed tests people are tempted to spend the last few seconds before time is called in marking answers at random – without even reading them – in the hope of picking up a few extra points. To discourage this practice, the instructions may warn you that your score will be "corrected" for guessing. That is, a penalty will be applied. The incorrect answers will be deducted from the correct ones, or some other penalty formula will be used.

9) **Review your answers**

If you finish before time is called, go back to the questions you guessed or omitted to give them further thought. Review other answers if you have time.

10) **Return your test materials**

If you are ready to leave before others have finished or time is called, take ALL your materials to the monitor and leave quietly. Never take any test material with you. The monitor can discover whose papers are not complete, and taking a test booklet may be grounds for disqualification.

VIII. EXAMINATION TECHNIQUES

1) Read the general instructions carefully. These are usually printed on the first page of the exam booklet. As a rule, these instructions refer to the timing of the examination; the fact that you should not start work until the signal and must stop work at a signal, etc. If there are any *special* instructions, such as a choice of questions to be answered, make sure that you note this instruction carefully.

2) When you are ready to start work on the examination, that is as soon as the signal has been given, read the instructions to each question booklet, underline any key words or phrases, such as *least, best, outline, describe* and the like. In this way you will tend to answer as requested rather than discover on reviewing your paper that you *listed without describing*, that you selected the *worst* choice rather than the *best* choice, etc.

3) If the examination is of the objective or multiple-choice type – that is, each question will also give a series of possible answers: A, B, C or D, and you are called upon to select the best answer and write the letter next to that answer on your answer paper – it is advisable to start answering each question in turn. There may be anywhere from 50 to 100 such questions in the three or four hours allotted and you can see how much time would be taken if you read through all the questions before beginning to answer any. Furthermore, if you come across a question or group of questions which you know would be difficult to answer, it would undoubtedly affect your handling of all the other questions.

4) If the examination is of the essay type and contains but a few questions, it is a moot point as to whether you should read all the questions before starting to answer any one. Of course, if you are given a choice – say five out of seven and the like – then it is essential to read all the questions so you can eliminate the two that are most difficult. If, however, you are asked to answer all the questions, there may be danger in trying to answer the easiest one first because you may find that you will spend too much time on it. The best technique is to answer the first question, then proceed to the second, etc.

5) Time your answers. Before the exam begins, write down the time it started, then add the time allowed for the examination and write down the time it must be completed, then divide the time available somewhat as follows:
   - If 3-1/2 hours are allowed, that would be 210 minutes. If you have 80 objective-type questions, that would be an average of 2-1/2 minutes per question. Allow yourself no more than 2 minutes per question, or a total of 160 minutes, which will permit about 50 minutes to review.
   - If for the time allotment of 210 minutes there are 7 essay questions to answer, that would average about 30 minutes a question. Give yourself only 25 minutes per question so that you have about 35 minutes to review.

6) The most important instruction is to *read each question* and make sure you know what is wanted. The second most important instruction is to *time yourself properly* so that you answer every question. The third most important instruction is to *answer every question*. Guess if you have to but include something for each question. Remember that you will receive no credit for a blank and will probably receive some credit if you write something in answer to an essay question. If you guess a letter – say "B" for a multiple-choice question – you may have guessed right. If you leave a blank as an answer to a multiple-choice question, the examiners may respect your feelings but it will not add a point to your score. Some exams may penalize you for wrong answers, so in such cases *only*, you may not want to guess unless you have some basis for your answer.

7) Suggestions
   a. Objective-type questions
      1. Examine the question booklet for proper sequence of pages and questions
      2. Read all instructions carefully
      3. Skip any question which seems too difficult; return to it after all other questions have been answered
      4. Apportion your time properly; do not spend too much time on any single question or group of questions

5. Note and underline key words – *all, most, fewest, least, best, worst, same, opposite,* etc.
6. Pay particular attention to negatives
7. Note unusual option, e.g., unduly long, short, complex, different or similar in content to the body of the question
8. Observe the use of "hedging" words – *probably, may, most likely,* etc.
9. Make sure that your answer is put next to the same number as the question
10. Do not second-guess unless you have good reason to believe the second answer is definitely more correct
11. Cross out original answer if you decide another answer is more accurate; do not erase until you are ready to hand your paper in
12. Answer all questions; guess unless instructed otherwise
13. Leave time for review

  b. Essay questions
   1. Read each question carefully
   2. Determine exactly what is wanted. Underline key words or phrases.
   3. Decide on outline or paragraph answer
   4. Include many different points and elements unless asked to develop any one or two points or elements
   5. Show impartiality by giving pros and cons unless directed to select one side only
   6. Make and write down any assumptions you find necessary to answer the questions
   7. Watch your English, grammar, punctuation and choice of words
   8. Time your answers; don't crowd material

8) Answering the essay question

Most essay questions can be answered by framing the specific response around several key words or ideas. Here are a few such key words or ideas:

M's: manpower, materials, methods, money, management
P's: purpose, program, policy, plan, procedure, practice, problems, pitfalls, personnel, public relations

  a. Six basic steps in handling problems:
   1. Preliminary plan and background development
   2. Collect information, data and facts
   3. Analyze and interpret information, data and facts
   4. Analyze and develop solutions as well as make recommendations
   5. Prepare report and sell recommendations
   6. Install recommendations and follow up effectiveness

  b. Pitfalls to avoid
   1. *Taking things for granted* – A statement of the situation does not necessarily imply that each of the elements is necessarily true; for example, a complaint may be invalid and biased so that all that can be taken for granted is that a complaint has been registered

2. *Considering only one side of a situation* – Wherever possible, indicate several alternatives and then point out the reasons you selected the best one
3. *Failing to indicate follow up* – Whenever your answer indicates action on your part, make certain that you will take proper follow-up action to see how successful your recommendations, procedures or actions turn out to be
4. *Taking too long in answering any single question* – Remember to time your answers properly

IX. AFTER THE TEST

Scoring procedures differ in detail among civil service jurisdictions although the general principles are the same. Whether the papers are hand-scored or graded by machine we have described, they are nearly always graded by number. That is, the person who marks the paper knows only the number – never the name – of the applicant. Not until all the papers have been graded will they be matched with names. If other tests, such as training and experience or oral interview ratings have been given, scores will be combined. Different parts of the examination usually have different weights. For example, the written test might count 60 percent of the final grade, and a rating of training and experience 40 percent. In many jurisdictions, veterans will have a certain number of points added to their grades.

After the final grade has been determined, the names are placed in grade order and an eligible list is established. There are various methods for resolving ties between those who get the same final grade – probably the most common is to place first the name of the person whose application was received first. Job offers are made from the eligible list in the order the names appear on it. You will be notified of your grade and your rank as soon as all these computations have been made. This will be done as rapidly as possible.

People who are found to meet the requirements in the announcement are called "eligibles." Their names are put on a list of eligible candidates. An eligible's chances of getting a job depend on how high he stands on this list and how fast agencies are filling jobs from the list.

When a job is to be filled from a list of eligibles, the agency asks for the names of people on the list of eligibles for that job. When the civil service commission receives this request, it sends to the agency the names of the three people highest on this list. Or, if the job to be filled has specialized requirements, the office sends the agency the names of the top three persons who meet these requirements from the general list.

The appointing officer makes a choice from among the three people whose names were sent to him. If the selected person accepts the appointment, the names of the others are put back on the list to be considered for future openings.

That is the rule in hiring from all kinds of eligible lists, whether they are for typist, carpenter, chemist, or something else. For every vacancy, the appointing officer has his choice of any one of the top three eligibles on the list. This explains why the person whose name is on top of the list sometimes does not get an appointment when some of the persons lower on the list do. If the appointing officer chooses the second or third eligible, the No. 1 eligible does not get a job at once, but stays on the list until he is appointed or the list is terminated.

X. HOW TO PASS THE INTERVIEW TEST

The examination for which you applied requires an oral interview test. You have already taken the written test and you are now being called for the interview test – the final part of the formal examination.

You may think that it is not possible to prepare for an interview test and that there are no procedures to follow during an interview. Our purpose is to point out some things you can do in advance that will help you and some good rules to follow and pitfalls to avoid while you are being interviewed.

What is an interview supposed to test?

The written examination is designed to test the technical knowledge and competence of the candidate; the oral is designed to evaluate intangible qualities, not readily measured otherwise, and to establish a list showing the relative fitness of each candidate – as measured against his competitors – for the position sought. Scoring is not on the basis of "right" and "wrong," but on a sliding scale of values ranging from "not passable" to "outstanding." As a matter of fact, it is possible to achieve a relatively low score without a single "incorrect" answer because of evident weakness in the qualities being measured.

Occasionally, an examination may consist entirely of an oral test – either an individual or a group oral. In such cases, information is sought concerning the technical knowledges and abilities of the candidate, since there has been no written examination for this purpose. More commonly, however, an oral test is used to supplement a written examination.

Who conducts interviews?

The composition of oral boards varies among different jurisdictions. In nearly all, a representative of the personnel department serves as chairman. One of the members of the board may be a representative of the department in which the candidate would work. In some cases, "outside experts" are used, and, frequently, a businessman or some other representative of the general public is asked to serve. Labor and management or other special groups may be represented. The aim is to secure the services of experts in the appropriate field.

However the board is composed, it is a good idea (and not at all improper or unethical) to ascertain in advance of the interview who the members are and what groups they represent. When you are introduced to them, you will have some idea of their backgrounds and interests, and at least you will not stutter and stammer over their names.

What should be done before the interview?

While knowledge about the board members is useful and takes some of the surprise element out of the interview, there is other preparation which is more substantive. It *is* possible to prepare for an oral interview – in several ways:

1) Keep a copy of your application and review it carefully before the interview

This may be the only document before the oral board, and the starting point of the interview. Know what education and experience you have listed there, and the sequence and dates of all of it. Sometimes the board will ask you to review the highlights of your experience for them; you should not have to hem and haw doing it.

2) Study the class specification and the examination announcement

Usually, the oral board has one or both of these to guide them. The qualities, characteristics or knowledges required by the position sought are stated in these documents. They offer valuable clues as to the nature of the oral interview. For example, if the job involves supervisory responsibilities, the announcement will usually indicate that knowledge of modern supervisory methods and the qualifications of the candidate as a supervisor will be tested. If so, you can expect such questions, frequently in the form of a hypothetical situation which you are expected to solve. NEVER go into an oral without knowledge of the duties and responsibilities of the job you seek.

3) Think through each qualification required

Try to visualize the kind of questions you would ask if you were a board member. How well could you answer them? Try especially to appraise your own knowledge and background in each area, *measured against the job sought*, and identify any areas in which you are weak. Be critical and realistic – do not flatter yourself.

4) Do some general reading in areas in which you feel you may be weak

For example, if the job involves supervision and your past experience has NOT, some general reading in supervisory methods and practices, particularly in the field of human relations, might be useful. Do NOT study agency procedures or detailed manuals. The oral board will be testing your understanding and capacity, not your memory.

5) Get a good night's sleep and watch your general health and mental attitude

You will want a clear head at the interview. Take care of a cold or any other minor ailment, and of course, no hangovers.

What should be done on the day of the interview?

Now comes the day of the interview itself. Give yourself plenty of time to get there. Plan to arrive somewhat ahead of the scheduled time, particularly if your appointment is in the fore part of the day. If a previous candidate fails to appear, the board might be ready for you a bit early. By early afternoon an oral board is almost invariably behind schedule if there are many candidates, and you may have to wait. Take along a book or magazine to read, or your application to review, but leave any extraneous material in the waiting room when you go in for your interview. In any event, relax and compose yourself.

The matter of dress is important. The board is forming impressions about you – from your experience, your manners, your attitude, and your appearance. Give your personal appearance careful attention. Dress your best, but not your flashiest. Choose conservative, appropriate clothing, and be sure it is immaculate. This is a business interview, and your appearance should indicate that you regard it as such. Besides, being well groomed and properly dressed will help boost your confidence.

Sooner or later, someone will call your name and escort you into the interview room. *This is it.* From here on you are on your own. It is too late for any more preparation. But remember, you asked for this opportunity to prove your fitness, and you are here because your request was granted.

What happens when you go in?

The usual sequence of events will be as follows: The clerk (who is often the board stenographer) will introduce you to the chairman of the oral board, who will introduce you to the other members of the board. Acknowledge the introductions before you sit down. Do not be surprised if you find a microphone facing you or a stenotypist sitting by. Oral interviews are usually recorded in the event of an appeal or other review.

Usually the chairman of the board will open the interview by reviewing the highlights of your education and work experience from your application – primarily for the benefit of the other members of the board, as well as to get the material into the record. Do not interrupt or comment unless there is an error or significant misinterpretation; if that is the case, do not hesitate. But do not quibble about insignificant matters. Also, he will usually ask you some question about your education, experience or your present job – partly to get you to start talking and to establish the interviewing "rapport." He may start the actual questioning, or turn it over to one of the other members. Frequently, each member undertakes the questioning on a particular area, one in which he is perhaps most competent, so you can expect each member to participate in the examination. Because time is limited, you may also expect some rather abrupt switches in the direction the questioning takes, so do not be upset by it. Normally, a board member will not pursue a single line of questioning unless he discovers a particular strength or weakness.

After each member has participated, the chairman will usually ask whether any member has any further questions, then will ask you if you have anything you wish to add. Unless you are expecting this question, it may floor you. Worse, it may start you off on an extended, extemporaneous speech. The board is not usually seeking more information. The question is principally to offer you a last opportunity to present further qualifications or to indicate that you have nothing to add. So, if you feel that a significant qualification or characteristic has been overlooked, it is proper to point it out in a sentence or so. Do not compliment the board on the thoroughness of their examination – they have been sketchy, and you know it. If you wish, merely say, "No thank you, I have nothing further to add." This is a point where you can "talk yourself out" of a good impression or fail to present an important bit of information. Remember, *you close the interview yourself*.

The chairman will then say, "That is all, Mr. _____, thank you." Do not be startled; the interview is over, and quicker than you think. Thank him, gather your belongings and take your leave. Save your sigh of relief for the other side of the door.

How to put your best foot forward

Throughout this entire process, you may feel that the board individually and collectively is trying to pierce your defenses, seek out your hidden weaknesses and embarrass and confuse you. Actually, this is not true. They are obliged to make an appraisal of your qualifications for the job you are seeking, and they want to see you in your best light. Remember, they must interview all candidates and a non-cooperative candidate may become a failure in spite of their best efforts to bring out his qualifications. Here are 15 suggestions that will help you:

1) Be natural – Keep your attitude confident, not cocky

If you are not confident that you can do the job, do not expect the board to be. Do not apologize for your weaknesses, try to bring out your strong points. The board is interested in a positive, not negative, presentation. Cockiness will antagonize any board member and make him wonder if you are covering up a weakness by a false show of strength.

2) Get comfortable, but don't lounge or sprawl

Sit erectly but not stiffly. A careless posture may lead the board to conclude that you are careless in other things, or at least that you are not impressed by the importance of the occasion. Either conclusion is natural, even if incorrect. Do not fuss with your clothing, a pencil or an ashtray. Your hands may occasionally be useful to emphasize a point; do not let them become a point of distraction.

3) Do not wisecrack or make small talk

This is a serious situation, and your attitude should show that you consider it as such. Further, the time of the board is limited – they do not want to waste it, and neither should you.

4) Do not exaggerate your experience or abilities

In the first place, from information in the application or other interviews and sources, the board may know more about you than you think. Secondly, you probably will not get away with it. An experienced board is rather adept at spotting such a situation, so do not take the chance.

5) If you know a board member, do not make a point of it, yet do not hide it

Certainly you are not fooling him, and probably not the other members of the board. Do not try to take advantage of your acquaintanceship – it will probably do you little good.

6) Do not dominate the interview

Let the board do that. They will give you the clues – do not assume that you have to do all the talking. Realize that the board has a number of questions to ask you, and do not try to take up all the interview time by showing off your extensive knowledge of the answer to the first one.

7) Be attentive

You only have 20 minutes or so, and you should keep your attention at its sharpest throughout. When a member is addressing a problem or question to you, give him your undivided attention. Address your reply principally to him, but do not exclude the other board members.

8) Do not interrupt

A board member may be stating a problem for you to analyze. He will ask you a question when the time comes. Let him state the problem, and wait for the question.

9) Make sure you understand the question

Do not try to answer until you are sure what the question is. If it is not clear, restate it in your own words or ask the board member to clarify it for you. However, do not haggle about minor elements.

10) Reply promptly but not hastily

A common entry on oral board rating sheets is "candidate responded readily," or "candidate hesitated in replies." Respond as promptly and quickly as you can, but do not jump to a hasty, ill-considered answer.

11) Do not be peremptory in your answers

A brief answer is proper – but do not fire your answer back. That is a losing game from your point of view. The board member can probably ask questions much faster than you can answer them.

12) Do not try to create the answer you think the board member wants

He is interested in what kind of mind you have and how it works – not in playing games. Furthermore, he can usually spot this practice and will actually grade you down on it.

13) Do not switch sides in your reply merely to agree with a board member

Frequently, a member will take a contrary position merely to draw you out and to see if you are willing and able to defend your point of view. Do not start a debate, yet do not surrender a good position. If a position is worth taking, it is worth defending.

14) Do not be afraid to admit an error in judgment if you are shown to be wrong

The board knows that you are forced to reply without any opportunity for careful consideration. Your answer may be demonstrably wrong. If so, admit it and get on with the interview.

15) Do not dwell at length on your present job

The opening question may relate to your present assignment. Answer the question but do not go into an extended discussion. You are being examined for a *new* job, not your present one. As a matter of fact, try to phrase ALL your answers in terms of the job for which you are being examined.

Basis of Rating

Probably you will forget most of these "do's" and "don'ts" when you walk into the oral interview room. Even remembering them all will not ensure you a passing grade. Perhaps you did not have the qualifications in the first place. But remembering them will help you to put your best foot forward, without treading on the toes of the board members.

Rumor and popular opinion to the contrary notwithstanding, an oral board wants you to make the best appearance possible. They know you are under pressure – but they also want to see how you respond to it as a guide to what your reaction would be under the pressures of the job you seek. They will be influenced by the degree of poise you display, the personal traits you show and the manner in which you respond.

ABOUT THIS BOOK

This book contains tests divided into Examination Sections. Go through each test, answering every question in the margin. We have also attached a sample answer sheet at the back of the book that can be removed and used. At the end of each test look at the answer key and check your answers. On the ones you got wrong, look at the right answer choice and learn. Do not fill in the answers first. Do not memorize the questions and answers, but understand the answer and principles involved. On your test, the questions will likely be different from the samples. Questions are changed and new ones added. If you understand these past questions you should have success with any changes that arise. Tests may consist of several types of questions. We have additional books on each subject should more study be advisable or necessary for you. Finally, the more you study, the better prepared you will be. This book is intended to be the last thing you study before you walk into the examination room. Prior study of relevant texts is also recommended. NLC publishes some of these in our Fundamental Series. Knowledge and good sense are important factors in passing your exam. Good luck also helps. So now study this Passbook, absorb the material contained within and take that knowledge into the examination. Then do your best to pass that exam.

EXAMINATION SECTION

EXAMINATION SECTION
TEST 1

DIRECTIONS: Each question or incomplete statement is followed by several suggested answers or completions. Select the one that BEST answers the question or completes the statement. *PRINT THE LETTER OF THE CORRECT ANSWER IN THE SPACE AT THE RIGHT.*

1. The process of building or improving a collection of library materials is known as
   A. collection development
   B. cataloging
   C. reader's advisory
   D. collection sourcing

   1._____

2. While working at the library circulation desk, a library assistant encounters a patron who is angry because a book he checked out is showing up as overdue when he is certain he has returned it. The patron begins yelling at her and, although she is maintaining a calm tone and demeanor, she is beginning to feel uncomfortable with the interaction. What should she do next?
   A. Call the police
   B. Call for backup from the person in charge
   C. Ban the patron from the library
   D. Remove the book from the patron's account

   2._____

3. In recent years, many libraries have adopted _____ technology, which uses radio waves that allow patrons to check out several items at once without opening or scanning them.
   A. Bluetooth   B. Cloud   C. RFID   D. LCD

   3._____

4. The American Library Association defines _____ as "documents which define the scope of a library's existing collections, plan for the continuing development of resources, identify collection strengths and outline the relationship between selection philosophy and the institution's goals, general selection criteria and intellectual freedom."
   A. card catalog records
   B. cataloging manuals
   C. reader's advisory policies
   D. collection development policies

   4._____

5. A library assistant is sometimes asked to go to a section of the stacks to make sure each item is in the proper order based upon call number. This is an important aspect of stack management known as
   A. shelf-reading
   B. copy cataloging
   C. book browsing
   D. shelf-shifting

   5._____

6. While libraries once used card catalogs to share library holdings information with library users, today libraries use _____ to do this.
   A. aggregator-neutral records (ANR)
   B. SQL cloud databases
   C. acquisition sections (AS)
   D. online public access catalogs (OPACs)

   6._____

1

7. Which of the following is NOT true of the Dewey Decimal Classification system?
   A. It is composed of 10 classes
   B. It is the classification system used in all academic libraries
   C. It is hierarchical in nature
   D. Each class in the system is composed of ten divisions

7.____

8. Which of the following is used by libraries to manage Internet access and comply with the Children Internet Protection Act?
   A. Anti-virus software
   B. Electronic reserves
   C. Internet filters
   D. OCLC database

8.____

9. While helping a patron check out, a library assistant notices that the patron is checking out one of her favorite books. What should the assistant do in this situation? She should
   A. comment on the book to create a sense of goodwill between her and the patron
   B. not comment on the book but make a mental note of the patron's selection so she can bring it up in future conversations
   C. comment on the book and recommend a few other books the patron might like based on his selection
   D. not comment on the book to maintain the patron's privacy

9.____

10. In the Dewey Decimal system, books related to the arts receive call numbers between _____ and _____.
    A. 700; 799
    B. 600; 699
    C. 100; 199
    D. 300; 399

10.____

11. While shelving books, a library assistant notices a patron walking through the stacks looking for a book. What should she do in this situation? She should
    A. stop shelving, greet the patron and ask if she needs help
    B. continue shelving books unless the patron requests her assistance
    C. smile at the patron and then, when she's done shelving, ask the patron if she needs assistance
    D. avoid making eye contact with the patron to ensure the patron's privacy

11.____

12. While he is working at the reference desk, a library assistant is asked by a patron where to find books about pets. How should he respond?
    A. By telling the patron that books about pets are located in the 630s
    B. By telling the patron that he can look up any book or subject on the catalog computer
    C. By asking the patron questions to determine more specifically what type of pet books the patron is looking for and then guiding him to them
    D. By calling a co-worker who is an avid pet lover to help the patron

12.____

13. Which call number would be MOST appropriate for a book about Zen Buddhism?
    A. 899.5
    B. 646.2
    C. 294.3
    D. 103.5

13.____

14. When a library assistant is helping a patron at the circulation desk, the patron asks to check out a reference book. The assistant knows that the library has a strict policy against checking out reference materials. What should she do in this situation?
    A. Ask the circulation manager if she can make an exception in this one case
    B. Recommend other options to the patron like photocopying the parts of the book the patron needs or finding a similar book in the circulating collection
    C. Tell the patron she is sorry but there is nothing she can do
    D. Tell the patron about the library's policy but agree to check the book out for him this one time

14.____

15. The Dewey Decimal system organizes items based upon
    A. title
    B. subject
    C. publication date
    D. author

15.____

16. When a library assistant calls a patron to inform him that a book he requested has arrived, the patron's wife answers and offers to take a message. What information should the assistant give to the patron's wife?
    A. "Your husband's copy of *The 4-Hour Work Week* has arrived, and it will be held for one week."
    B. "An item your husband requested has arrived, and if he wants more information, he should call the library directly."
    C. "Your husband's copy of *The 4-Hour Work Week* has arrived, and we expect his copy of *The 4-Hour Body* to arrive tomorrow."
    D. "A book has arrived for your husband, and we will hold it for one week."

16.____

17. In a library, the act of adding an item to the library catalog, including a bibliographic description and classification, is known as
    A. cataloging
    B. indexing
    C. bibliographic processing
    D. descriptive linking

17.____

18. While checking in items at the circulation desk, a library assistant comes across a book with very loose binding and several pages falling out. He also notices that a patron has a hold on this particular title. What should he do?
    He should check the book in and then
    A. put it on hold for the patron
    B. follow his library's procedure for sending a book to the bindery for repair, as well as request a copy of the book from another library for the patron waiting
    C. call the patron who is waiting for the book and ask her whether she would rather take the book as it is or wait until it is repaired
    D. withdraw the book from the catalog and throw it away

18.____

4 (#1)

19. On occasions where it is necessary for library staff to make a notation in a book, this should be done
    A. with a bold marker to ensure that the notation is seen
    B. with a pen that matches the color of the book's font
    C. lightly, with a soft pencil to prevent any indentations
    D. with a typed label created in a labelmaker

    19._____

20. Which of the following is TRUE about the proper procedure for handling audio-visual materials such as CDs, DVDs and Blu-ray discs?
    A. They should only be handled by touching the edges and the center hole
    B. They can be touched anywhere as long as they are cleaned regularly
    C. They should never be touched unless you are wearing gloves
    D. Any visible scratches should be buffed out with a moist paper towel

    20._____

21. Which of the following behaviors represents the proper use of a photocopier in a library?
    A. Photocopying a very old, rare book
    B. Photocopying a book by laying it flat on the glass and pressing down on the spine so you can copy two pages at a time
    C. Photocopying a book one page at a time by placing half of the book on the glass and supporting the rest of the book with your hand
    D. Photocopying the loose pages of a book with a broken spine just in case the pages go missing

    21._____

22. A library's _____ includes books and other items that are housed separately from the main collection due to their rarity, value, condition, subject or history.
    A. serial collection   B. archives
    C. reference section   D. special collections

    22._____

23. When Mr. Buckley, a regular patron at Elm Park Library, registers for a library program called "Surviving Divorce," a library assistant says to his co-worker, "Did you see that Mr. Buckley registered for the divorce program: No wonder I haven't seen Mrs. Buckley around lately." Considering that he is a professional library worker, what is wrong with the assistant's comment?
    A. He is impinging upon the patron's right to intellectual freedom
    B. He is not fulfilling his responsibility to maintain the patron's confidentiality
    C. He is speculating about the patron's relationship without any concrete facts
    D. He is slandering the patron and could be sued for defamation

    23._____

24. While a library assistant is working at the circulation desk, a distraught patron comes to the desk with a stack of books and explains that he forgot his library card at home but really needs the books for a paper he is working on that is due tomorrow. The patron is worried because the library is closing in ten minutes, and he won't have time to go home and get his card. What should the assistant do in this situation?
    A. Ask the patron for a photo I.D. so she can pull up his account manually and check out the books

    24._____

B. Ask the patron for his name so she can pull up his account manually and check out the books
C. Ask the patron for his library card number so she can pull up his account manually and check out the books
D. Tell the patron that there is nothing she can do and that if he wants the books he will have to return tomorrow

25. Most libraries in the United States use either the Dewey Decimal system or the _____ Classification system for classifying and organizing library materials. 25._____
    A. Colon
    B. Library of Congress
    C. Bliss
    D. Universal Decimal

KEY (CORRECT ANSWERS)

1.	A		11.	A
2.	B		12.	C
3.	C		13.	C
4.	D		14.	B
5.	A		15.	B
6.	D		16.	D
7.	B		17.	A
8.	C		18.	B
9.	D		19.	C
10.	A		20.	A

21. C
22. D
23. B
24. A
25. B

TEST 2

DIRECTIONS: Each question or incomplete statement is followed by several suggested answers or completions. Select the one that BEST answers the question or completes the statement. *PRINT THE LETTER OF THE CORRECT ANSWER IN THE SPACE AT THE RIGHT.*

1. Which of the following is TRUE of caring for water-damaged books? 1.____
   A. All types of books can be air-dried with good results
   B. Wet books should never be laid flat to air-dry because it promotes mold growth
   C. Paper towels tend to further damage books and should not be used to dry wet books
   D. Water-damaged books with glossy pages, leather or parchment should be immediately frozen

2. Public libraries typically require a _____ for library card registration. 2.____
   A. current photo ID that includes the individual's name and address
   B. current photo ID and three personal references
   C. background and credit check
   D. birth certificate or Social Security card

3. Although library directors are typically the top authority in a library, most libraries are ultimately controlled by the 3.____
   A. taxpayers   B. board of trustees
   C. reference department   D. technical services department

4. All of the following are functions of the Technical Services Department EXCEPT 4.____
   A. cataloging   B. processing
   C. acquisitions   D. reader's advisory

5. A(n) _____ is a software program used by libraries to automate functions such as cataloging, circulation, serials, acquisitions and the online catalog for library patrons. 5.____
   A. online public access catalog (OPAC)
   B. open source reporting system (OSRS)
   C. integrated library system (ILS)
   D. multiuser automated database (MAD)

6. While working at the reference desk, a library assistant gets caught in a lengthy conversation with a patron about his favorite author and why his first book is better than his second book. The assistant can tell the patron is lonely and looking for someone to talk to, but other patrons are also waiting for her help. What should she do in this situation? 6.____
   She should
   A. continue talking to the patron while giving him behavioral clues, like looking at the clock, to suggest she needs to end the conversation

B. be blunt with the patron and tell him he is taking up too much of her time, otherwise he will continue to do so in the future
C. politely tell the patron she has to help the other patrons in line, but suggest that he participate in some of the library's clubs and events where he can talk to others who share his love of books
D. tell the patron to wait a minute, quickly help the other patrons in line, and then return to the conversation so as not to be rude

7. In the Library of Congress Classification system, the main classes are designated by
   A. letters of the alphabet
   B. special characters
   C. a three-digit code
   D. the author's last name

8. A library assistant works in the acquisitions unit and is asked by the director to order a replacement for a damaged book that was published in 1979. While searching for the book, he realizes that it is out-of-print. What should he do in this situation?
   A. Tell the director he can't order it
   B. Order it through a retailer, like Amazon, that often carries out-of-print items
   C. Order it through a wholesaler, like Baker & Taylor, that often carries out-of-print items
   D. Offer to buy it from another library that owns it

9. Who is typically the final decision maker when it comes to collection development in a library?
   A. The technical services manager
   B. The acquisition assistant
   C. The head reference librarian
   D. The library director

10. While working at the reference desk, a library assistant is approached by a patron who complains that another patron is talking very loudly on her cellphone in a quiet reading area. When the assistant asks the patron if she can take her call outside, the patron refuses and continues talking. How should the assistant handle this situation?
    She should
    A. forcibly confiscate the cellphone from the patron
    B. return to the reference desk and tell the patron who complained that she's sorry but there is nothing else she can do
    C. call her manager or the library director and have him or her ask the patron to take the call outside; if the patron still refuses, they can call the police
    D. grab the patron by the arm and escort her out of the building

11. All of the following are examples of e-resources EXCEPT
    A. microforms
    B. databases
    C. web resource links
    D. streaming media

12. Which call number would be MOST appropriate for a travel guide about Hawaii?
    A. 919.69
    B. 747.13
    C. 316.45
    D. 103.25

13. Public libraries receive most of their funding from which of the following sources? 13.____
    A. Individual donations
    B. State and local government
    C. Corporate donations
    D. Endowments

14. When processing books, library workers should always make sure to 14.____
    A. use a ballpoint pen to mark them
    B. attach notes to them with paperclips or rubber bands
    C. stack them with the smallest ones on the bottom and the biggest ones on the top
    D. use plain, acid-free paper for place markers or notes

15. Which of the following is NOT a fundamental characteristic of all public libraries? 15.____
    A. They are voluntary in nature, unlike public schools
    B. They provide most services free of charge
    C. They are open to most groups, except groups that are known to be discriminatory or controversial
    D. They are established by state law

16. While an assistant is working at the reference desk, a patron approaches her and asks her to help him on the computer. The patron had been working on a research paper when the computer crashed. He believes he might have lost half of his work, but he is hoping the assistant can help him access the work he lost. She follows the patron to his computer to see what she can do, but she is unable to figure out how to access the lost information. What should she say in this circumstance? 16.____
    A. "I'm sorry, but I haven't been able to find your lost work so far. Let me contact our IT specialist and see if she has any suggestions."
    B. "I haven't found your lost information, but I'm 100% positive it's here. So don't worry, I will definitely find it for you."
    C. "No one has ever had this problem with this computer before. What were you doing before it crashed?"
    D. "There's nothing I can do. You should have saved it more frequently."

17. Which of the following is TRUE of the Library of Congress Classification (LCC) system as compared to the Dewey Decimal Classification (DDC) system? 17.____
    A. The LCC system does not use cutter numbers, whereas the DDC system does
    B. The LCC system has more numbers and more specific classes than the DDC
    C. LCC call numbers are usually longer than DDC call numbers of the same specificity
    D. The LCC system tends to be easier to browse from a subject searcher's perspective

18. Which of the following BEST describes MARC formats?   18.____
    A. A set of cataloging rules   B. A cataloging code
    C. A computer system   D. A set of mark-up protocols

19. While working at the reference desk, an assistant receives a call from a patron who   19.____
    wants more information on a special display that is set up in the Youth Services
    Department. How should he handle this request?
    He should
    A. tell the patron to hold and transfer her to Youth Services
    B. tell the patron everything he knows about the display and then suggest
       that if the patron wants to know more, she should call back and enter the
       extension for Youth Services
    C. tell the patron that he is going to transfer her to the librarian on-duty in
       Youth Services. He should also give the patron his name and extension
       just in case the patron gets disconnected
    D. take a message and tell the patron he will have the librarian in charge of
       the display call her back when she comes in for her next shift tomorrow

20. Which of the following is TRUE about the application of copyright law in   20.____
    libraries?
    A. The first sale doctrine allows libraries to lend books and other resources
       that are copyrighted
    B. Fair use frees libraries from any liability or responsibility when it comes to
       copyright regulations
    C. Copyright law prohibits libraries from reproducing copyrighted works for
       users with disabilities
    D. Libraries are not allowed to reproduce copyrighted works, even if it's for
       preservation and replacement purposes

21. Which of the following behaviors BEST demonstrates the American Library   21.____
    Association's "Poor People's Policy"?
    A. Asking a homeless patron not to sleep in the library because it makes
       other patrons uncomfortable
    B. Requiring proof of address for library card registration
    C. Hiring a security guard in an attempt to balance the need for open access
       with the need for safety
    D. Removing fees and overdue charges that can act as an access barrier to
       economically challenged patrons

22. In the Library of Congress Classification system, a book about philosophy   22.____
    would be in a class designated by _____, whereas in the Dewey Decimal
    Classification system, it would be in a class designated by
    A. the number 200; the letter A   B. the number 100; the letter B
    C. the letter A; the number 200   D. the letter B; the number 100

23. An assistant is helping a patron who needs a book as soon as possible for a research project. The book, however, is already checked out to another patron and is not owned by any other libraries. What action should the assistant take?
    A. None; there is nothing he can do in this circumstance
    B. He should recall the book, which will require the patron who has it checked out to return it sooner
    C. He should place a hold on the book in hopes that the patron who has it checked out will realize that someone else is waiting for it and return it sooner
    D. He should call the patron who has it checked out and request that she return it immediately

24. Which of the following technologies is being adopted by many libraries as an alternative to barcodes?
    A. Accession records
    B. MARC records
    C. RFID tags
    D. RLG sensors

25. While an assistant is working at the circulation desk, a patron approaches him with a book she would like to check out but tells him she is from out of town and only has a library card from her own library. Which library program should he introduce the patron to?
    A. Interlibrary loan
    B. Reciprocal borrowing
    C. Document delivery
    D. Homebound services

KEY (CORRECT ANSWERS)

1.	D	11.	A
2.	A	12.	A
3.	B	13.	B
4.	D	14.	D
5.	C	15.	C
6.	C	16.	A
7.	A	17.	B
8.	B	18.	D
9.	D	19.	C
10.	C	20.	A

21. D
22. D
23. B
24. C
25. B

TEST 3

DIRECTIONS: Each question or incomplete statement is followed by several suggested answers or completions. Select the one that BEST answers the question or completes the statement. *PRINT THE LETTER OF THE CORRECT ANSWER IN THE SPACE AT THE RIGHT.*

1. Which of the following terms is used to describe groups of libraries that participate in cooperative resource purchasing and sharing? 1.____
   A. Consortia
   B. Integrated library systems
   C. Public access systems
   D. Resource associations

2. An assistant works in the Archives Department of an academic library and is often handling delicate historical books and documents. Which of the following behaviors should she NEVER engage in? 2.____
   A. Stacking oversized books on the bottom shelf so they don't protrude
   B. Using post-it notes to indicate when a book needs to be repaired
   C. Pulling books off the shelf from the spine with her fingers on the boards
   D. Washing her hands before handling library materials

3. All of the following components are usually included in an integrated library system EXCEPT a(n) _____ module. 3.____
   A. acquisitions   B. serials   C. cataloging   D. marketing

4. Which of the following is an example of proper library customer service over the phone? 4.____
   A. Telling a patron you are transferring him or her to another department before doing so
   B. Transferring a patron to another department without telling your co-worker what the patron's question is in order to save time
   C. Asking patrons to repeat their questions several times to ensure you answer them correctly
   D. Telling a patron you will call him back if you are too busy, but not specifying when since you don't know exactly when you'll have time

5. Which of the following call numbers would be MOST appropriate for a book about holiday baking? 5.____
   A. 824.13HOL   B. 641.865HOL   C. 691.476BAK   D. 194.634MAK

6. While working at the reference desk, a patron approaches an assistant to tell him that a book he is looking for is not on the shelf where it is supposed to be. The assistant pulls up the book's record in the online catalog and the catalog shows that the book should be on the shelf. What is the next step he should take in this situation? 6.____
   He should
   A. change the book's status to "missing"
   B. check the hold shelf for the book
   C. check the shelf himself to make sure the book is not there
   D. request a copy of the book from another library for the patron

7. What aspect of collection management must be implemented when a section of a collection is full and there is no longer room for new titles in this section?
   A. Shelf reading
   B. Cataloging
   C. Shifting
   D. Reader's advisory

7.____

8. An assistant's manager gives him a list of items that need to be withdrawn from the library's collection to make room for new titles. This process is known as
   A. weeding
   B. processing
   C. shelf reading
   D. deleting

8.____

9. Which of the following technologies is used by libraries, particularly newer academic libraries, to store large amounts of library items in a densely packed off-site location?
   A. Integrated library storage systems
   B. Automated storage and retrieval systems
   C. Consortia warehouses
   D. Radio frequency identification

9.____

10. All of the following have an impact on a library's public relations (PR) EXCEPT
    A. how employees answer the telephone
    B. how many items are improperly shelved
    C. the presence of clear and useful signage
    D. the number of members on the Board of Trustees

10.____

11. Which of the following is TRUE of trade publishers?
    A. The only publish non-fiction
    B. They sell to three primary markets: libraries, bookstores and wholesalers
    C. Their price is lower than other publishers due to mass sales
    D. They only publish fiction

11.____

12. Newspapers, magazines, newsletters and journals are all examples of _____ publications carried by libraries.
    A. database
    B. mass-market
    C. serial
    D. trade

12.____

13. An assistant is helping a patron who is required to perform research using journals for a school paper. The paper must be on a topic related to the town's local history. What subcategory of journals would be MOST useful to this patron?
    A. Parochial journals
    B. Practical professional journals
    C. Primary and secondary research journals
    D. Nonspecialized journals for intellectuals

13.____

14. All of the following are typical methods for organizing journals and magazines in libraries EXCEPT 14.____
    A. alphabetically by title
    B. alphabetically by title within larger subject groupings
    C. alphabetically by publisher
    D. using the same classification system as books in the collection

15. An assistant is overseeing a shifting project in two major subject areas. What final step should he implement before the project is complete? 15.____
    A. The installation of bigger shelving units
    B. A thorough shelf reading
    C. The shifting of the subject sections immediately before and after the sections being shifted
    D. The creation of new shelving labels

16. While an assistant is working at the reference desk, a patron approaches him with a book she has been using for in-library research and asks him what she should do with the book now that she is done with it. What is the MOST appropriate response in this situation? 16.____
    He should
    A. tell the patron to return the book to the shelf where she found it
    B. tell the patron to put the book on one of the shelving carts located in the stacks
    C. tell the patron to put the book in the return drop at the circulation desk
    D. take the book from the patron and leave the reference desk to return the book to the shelf himself

17. While an assistant is working at the reference desk, a patron asks him for help locating a recent report published by the USDA. Where should he direct this patron? 17.____
    A. To the federal government's web portal USA.gov
    B. To the library's in-house government document archive
    C. To a Federal Depository Library Program (FDLP) library
    D. To their local village hall

18. If a patron asked for help finding a primary source for a school paper, which of the following would suffice? 18.____
    A. A television documentary on DVD
    B. An encyclopedia
    C. A historical diary found in the library's archives
    D. A peer-reviewed journal article

19. What is the PRIMARY factor used to determine whether an item is included in a library's archives or special collections? 19.____
    A. Whether the item is in high demand
    B. Whether it's owned by any other libraries
    C. Its age – only items over 30 years old should be included in these sections
    D. Whether it requires special care to ensure long-term preservation

20. An assistant was recently hired as a cataloging assistant and is cataloging her first 20.____
book, which is a newly acquired title that is on the New York Times bestsellers
list. Which of the following steps should she take FIRST?
   A. Decide upon a call number for the book
   B. Create an original record
   C. Search for an existing record she can copy
   D. Cover and label the book

Questions 21-25.

DIRECTIONS: In answering Questions 21 through 25, match the call number in Column A to its proper place on a library shelf in Column B.

Column A		Column B	
21. 654.1678BEA	A.	First	21.____
22. 654.93ALG	B.	Second	22.____
23. 645.1GOR	C.	Third	23.____
24. 654.167CAL	D.	Fourth	24.____
25. 654BEC	E.	Fifth	

KEY (CORRECT ANSWERS)

1.	A		11.	B
2.	B		12.	C
3.	D		13.	A
4.	A		14.	C
5.	B		15.	B
6.	C		16.	B
7.	C		17.	A
8.	A		18.	C
9.	B		19.	D
10.	D		20.	C

21.	D
22.	E
23.	A
24.	C
25.	B

TEST 4

DIRECTIONS: Each question or incomplete statement is followed by several suggested answers or completions. Select the one that BEST answers the question or completes the statement. *PRINT THE LETTER OF THE CORRECT ANSWER IN THE SPACE AT THE RIGHT.*

1. A library assistant is asked by her manager to give direction to a volunteer who is working at the library to fulfill community service requirements. The assistant has a lot of work to accomplish and is trying to decide which task would be the best to assign to the volunteer.
   Which of the following would be the BEST choice based upon the fact that the volunteer has no previous library experience and the assistant has little time to train him?
   Asking the volunteer to
   A. follow-up with a patron who left a message about a lost book
   B. re-shelve books that has just been repaired
   C. affix pre-made labels to items that have just been cataloged
   D. perform copy cataloging on newly received items

   1.____

2. A useful reference book has all of the following characteristics EXCEPT
   A. tiny typeface
   B. photographs and illustrations
   C. relevant cross-references
   D. an index with indented subheadings

   2.____

3. Which of the following is considered a secondary source?
   A. A journal article   B. An interview
   C. A manuscript   D. A photograph

   3.____

4. Which of the following is NOT a responsibility of a library's Board of Trustees?
   A. Appointing a library director
   B. Adopting an annual budget
   C. Creating written policies that govern library operations
   D. Identifying candidates and approving the selection of library staff

   4.____

5. While an assistant is working at the reference desk, a patron approaches her with his teenage son and tells her that he caught his son reading a book from the Young Adult collection that is inappropriate for someone his age. How should the assistant respond?
   A. By telling the patron he is out of line and is trying to impede upon First Amendment rights
   B. By telling the patron that if he doesn't like the library's collection, he is free to go elsewhere for books
   C. By apologizing to the patron and telling him she will remove the book from the collection immediately
   D. By telling the patron that she is sorry that he found the book upsetting and asking him if she can help and find something more acceptable for his son to read

   5.____

6. What database would be MOST helpful to a patron writing a paper for a master's level course in educational leadership?
   A. HeritageQuest B. LexisNexis
   C. ERIC D. Novelist Plus

7. While working in the Youth Services Department, an assistant notices that an older male patron is periodically staring at a child in a way that she finds suspicious. She is certain that this patron is not the child's parent or guardian because she saw the child enter the library with someone else. What should she do in this circumstance?
   A. Ask the patron to leave the department immediately, and if he doesn't, call the police
   B. Approach the patron and ask him if she can help him with anything. Regardless of his response, she should check in with the patron and ask if he needs help, to remind him of her presence. She can also keep an eye on him until he leaves the department.
   C. Ask her manager to come and address the situation. Serious situations should be left to the librarian in charge.
   D. Ask the patron directly why he is staring at the child and, depending on his response, take appropriate action, which may include police intervention or a lifetime ban from the library.

8. While she is working at the reference desk, an assistant is approached by a patron who asks for a book recommendation. The patron has just read the book *Big Magic* by Elizabeth Gilbert and wants to read something similar, but by a different author since he has already read all of Elizabeth Gilbert's books. The assistant is not familiar with this book and is at a loss for what to recommend. What should she do?
   A. Look up a description of the book, and if she still can't think of anything, enter the title into a database like Novelist Plus to see what it recommends.
   B. Recommend some of her own favorite books, even if they might not be similar.
   C. Call the reader's advisory librarian at home to ask for a recommendation.
   D. Tell the patron she is sorry but he will have to return to the library at another time for a recommendation.

9. Which, among the following library staff positions, typically has the MOST authority and would make operational decisions when a director or manager is not present?
   A. Library assistant B. Library page
   C. Reference librarian D. Administrative assistant

10. Which of the following databases would be MOST useful to a patron looking to access a newspaper article from 1998?
    A. Standard & Poor's Net Advantage B. General OneFile
    C. Gale Virtual Reference Library D. Novelist Plus

Questions 11-14.

DIRECTIONS: In answering Questions 11 through 14, match the library type in Column A with the description that MOST accurately describes it in Column B.

	Column A		Column B	
11.	Special Library	A.	A library that serves students in Grades K-12	11.____
12.	Public Library	B.	A library that serves a clientele in a particular niche	12.____
13.	Academic Library	C.	A library associated with a university or college	13.____
14.	School Library	D.	A library that serves members of a community	14.____

15. _____ refers to subject headings or terms selected by indexers to describe a concept and make searches easier and more relevant.
    A. Alt text
    B. Abbreviated entry
    C. Keyword vocabulary
    D. Controlled vocabulary

15.____

16. In most libraries, collection development is based on
    A. the preferences of its librarians
    B. directives from the American Library Association
    C. the priorities established in the library's Collection Development Policy
    D. the direction of the Board of Trustees

16.____

17. Which of the following is an example of a tertiary source?
    A. An encyclopedia
    B. An interview
    C. A journal article
    D. A letter

17.____

18. When you search a database using your own vocabulary, you are performing a _____ search.
    A. controlled vocabulary
    B. keyword
    C. accession
    D. full text

18.____

19. Which of the following is the oldest and largest library association in the world?
    A. The International Association of University Libraries
    B. The American Library Association (ALA)
    C. The Online Computer Library Center (OCLC)
    D. The Medical Library Association

19.____

20. Which of the following is TRUE of RDA cataloging rules versus AACR2 cataloging rules?
    A. RDA generally avoids the use of abbreviations.
    B. RDA uses varied systems of measurement for an item's dimensions depending on the type of resource.
    C. RDA uses the term "heading" as opposed to AACR2's term "authorized access point."
    D. RDA does not differentiate between recording and transcribing elements.

20.____

Questions 21-25.

DIRECTIONS: In answering Questions 21 through 25, match the library book in Column A to the best fitting genre in Column B.

Column A

Column B

21. A factual book recounting the life of James Brown

A. Autobiography
B. Science fiction
C. Non-fiction
D. Historical fiction
E. Biography

21.____

22. A book set during the Holocaust with imaginary characters

22.____

23. A book set on an imaginary planet

23.____

24. A factual book about the American healthcare system

24.____

25. A book written by Nelson Mandela about his own life

25.____

KEY (CORRECT ANSWERS)

1.	C	11.	B
2.	A	12.	D
3.	A	13.	C
4.	D	14.	A
5.	D	15.	D
6.	C	16.	C
7.	B	17.	A
8.	A	18.	B
9.	C	19.	B
10.	B	20.	A

21. E
22. D
23. B
24. C
25. A

EXAMINATION SECTION
TEST 1

DIRECTIONS: Each question or incomplete statement is followed by several suggested answers or completions. Select the one that BEST answers the question or completes the statement. *PRINT THE LETTER OF THE CORRECT ANSWER IN THE SPACE AT THE RIGHT.*

1. A book about the life of another person is called a(n)

    A. monograph B. fiction C. biography
    D. autobiography E. reference

    1._____

2. A book about real experiences is usually referred to as a(n)

    A. reference B. monograph C. fiction
    D. non-fiction E. autobiography

    2._____

3. The Dewey Decimal system is a

    A. list of books, magazines, and non-print materials
    B. system for checking out books
    C. method for organizing materials
    D. system for filing cards
    E. system for networking

    3._____

4. A catalog card reading MOVIE see MOTION PICTURE means:

    A. All books on movies will be found under the subject heading MOTION PICTURE
    B. Additional books on movies will be found under the subject heading MOTION PICTURE
    C. Another library has the motion picture holdings
    D. Materials are expected on motion pictures
    E. All materials on movies are circulating

    4._____

5. A bibliography is a(n)

    A. encyclopedia B. networking
    C. means of circulating materials D. list of materials
    E. reference tool

    5._____

6. An annotation is a(n)

    A. review B. explanatory note C. precis
    D. format E. critique

    6._____

7. AMERICAN REFERENCE BOOKS ANNUAL provides a

    A. comprehensive reviewing service of reference books published in the United States
    B. monthly periodical furnishing reviews of popular reference tools
    C. publisher's guide to monthly reviewing sources
    D. professional journal published by the American Library Association
    E. bibliography of bibliographies

    7._____

8. An index is a(n)

   A. table of contents
   B. encyclopedia
   C. series of footnotes
   D. bibliography
   E. guide to locate material

9. The library catalog is a(n)

   A. shelf list
   B. index to the materials collection
   C. bibliography
   D. system for reserves
   E. collection of book orders

10. A shelf list is a

    A. record of materials in a library
    B. reserve list
    C. weeding list
    D. list of reference materials
    E. bibliography of reference sources

11. Technical services include

    A. acquisitions, cataloging, and materials preparation
    B. reference work and user services
    C. reader's advisory services
    D. circulation and reference services
    E. networking

12. A collection of materials such as pamphlets, clippings, or illustrations kept in special containers is referred to as a

    A. card catalog
    B. card file
    C. vertical file
    D. container collection
    E. clipping file

13. An electromagnetic recording made for playback on a television set is referred to as a(n)

    A. audio tape
    B. cassette
    C. video-recording
    D. superdisk
    E. fiche

14. A word, name, object, group of words, or acronym describing a subject is usually referred to as a

    A. cross reference
    B. subject heading
    C. nom de plume
    D. serial
    E. catalog card

15. A collection of materials with restricted circulation usually found in college and university libraries is called a(n) _____ collection.

    A. reserved materials
    B. patron
    C. student
    D. open stack
    E. rotating reserve

16. An independent publication of forty-nine pages or less, bound in paper covers, is called a

    A. serial
    B. monograph
    C. microcard
    D. pamphlet
    E. fiche

17. Library work directly concerned with assistance to readers in securing information and in using library resources is termed

    A. circulation services
    B. technical services
    C. reader's advisory services
    D. user services
    E. networking

18. A three-dimensional representation of a real object reproduced in the original size or to scale is called a(n)

    A. model
    B. film
    C. microform
    D. ultrafiche
    E. videotape

19. The act of filling out required forms to become an eligible library borrower is called

    A. serialization
    B. direction
    C. registration
    D. reference work
    E. signing

20. A direction in a catalog that guides the user to related names or subjects is termed a _____ reference.

    A. shelf
    B. see-also
    C. title
    D. see
    E. subject

21. A record of a work in the catalog under the title is called a

    A. subject card
    B. number entry
    C. author card
    D. subject entry
    E. title entry

22. The printed scheme of a classification system is referred to as a

    A. classification schedule
    B. numbering schedule
    C. lettering schedule
    D. cutter number
    E. copyright

23. The entry of a work in the catalog under the subject heading is called a

    A. subject card
    B. subject heading
    C. subject entry
    D. reference entry
    E. subject guide

24. The department in a library responsible for officially listing prospective borrowers is the _____ department.

    A. reference
    B. registration
    C. welcoming
    D. circulation
    E. technical

25. Library work that deals with patrons and the use of the library collection is called _____ services.

    A. technical
    B. reader
    C. circulation
    D. reference
    E. public

KEY (CORRECT ANSWERS)

1. C	11. A
2. D	12. C
3. C	13. C
4. A	14. B
5. D	15. A
6. B	16. D
7. A	17. D
8. E	18. A
9. B	19. C
10. A	20. B

21. E
22. A
23. C
24. B
25. D

TEST 2

DIRECTIONS: Each question or incomplete statement is followed by several suggested answers or completions. Select the one that BEST answers the question or completes the statement. *PRINT THE LETTER OF THE CORRECT ANSWER IN THE SPACE AT THE RIGHT.*

1. Material held for a borrower for a limited time is termed _____ material.

   A. reference B. reserved C. circulation
   D. special   E. held

2. A notice sent to a borrower to remind him to return heldover due material is a(n)

   A. warning   B. notice   C. overdue notice
   D. warning notice E. call slip

3. Material returned to the library before the date due is

   A. Penalized B. returned   C. accepted
   D. unneeded   E. subject to examination

4. Real objects, specimens, or artifacts are called

   A. toys   B. realia C. games
   D. opaque material E. models

5. A film with a series of pictures in sequence which creates the illusion of motion when projected is classified as a

   A. photogram B. motion picture C. videotape
   D. cassette   E. slide

6. Laying books on the shelves in proper order is called

   A. placing B. weeding C. reading D. shifting E. shelving

7. A publication issued in successive parts usually to be continued indefinitely is referred to as a

   A. paper B. monograph C. serial D. pamphlet E. edition

8. A record of the loan of material is called a

   A. call slip B. reserve C. contract D. copy E. charge

9. Information arranged in tabular, outline, or graphic form on a sheet of paper is called a

   A. classification B. charge   C. chart
   D. catalog   E. cartoon

10. The method used to lend materials to borrowers and maintain the necessary records is the _____ system.

    A. classification B. circulation control C. reference
    D. borrowing   E. returnable

11. Any entry, other than a subject entry, that is made in a catalog in addition to the main entry is called a(n)

    A. added entry   B. call number   C. central reference
    D. reference entry   E. explanatory entry

12. The record of the number of items charged out of a library is termed

    A. record statistics   B. circulation statistics
    C. circulation control   D. record control
    E. itemizing

13. A number assigned to each book or item as it is received by the library is referred to as a(n) _____ number.

    A. call   B. accession   C. entry
    D. acquisition   E. ordering

14. A master file of all registered borrowers in a library system is called the _____ file.

    A. personnel   B. charging   C. classification
    D. central registration   E. circulation control

15. A person who charges out materials from a library is called the

    A. lender   B. technician   C. professional librarian
    D. clerk   E. borrower

16. A catalog in which all entries are filed in alphabetical order is called a(n) _____ catalog.

    A. card   B. Library of Congress   C. alphabetical
    D. dictionary   E. subject

17. The day material is to be returned to a library is usually referred to as the _____ day.

    A. library   B. date-due   C. return
    D. book   E. library-due

18. The act of annulling the library's record of a loan is called

    A. discharging   B. cancelling   C. stamping
    D. recording   E. unloaning

19. The penalty charge for material returned after the date due is called a(n)

    A. charge   B. fine   C. tax   D. levy   E. arrangement

20. A set of materials containing rules designed to be played in a competitive situation is called a

    A. rolodome   B. game   C. sketch   D. linedex   E. materialsset

21. A catalog in more than one part is termed a _____ catalog.

    A. divided   B. split   C. Library of Congress
    D. Dewey   E. Sears

22. A metal file containing a number of flat metal leaves that hold single cardboard strips list- 22.____
    ing titles and holdings is called a

    A. linedesk   B. linetop   C. rolotop
    D. rotofile   E. linedex

23. A metal file containing a number of shallow drawers in which serial check-in cards are 23.____
    kept is usually referred to as a

    A. linedesk   B. rotofile   C. box   D. kardex   E. linetop

24. The strip of paper pasted in the book or on the book packet, on which the date due is 24.____
    stamped, is called the

    A. date slip   B. date card   C. date strip
    D. call slip   E. card strip

25. Film on which materials have been photographed in greatly reduced size is called 25.____

    A. minifilm   B. microfilm   C. photogram
    D. miniaturization E. photoreduction

KEY (CORRECT ANSWERS)

1.	B	11.	A
2.	C	12.	B
3.	C	13.	B
4.	B	14.	D
5.	B	15.	E
6.	E	16.	D
7.	C	17.	B
8.	E	18.	A
9.	C	19.	B
10.	B	20.	B

21. A
22. E
23. D
24. A
25. B

EXAMINATION SECTION
TEST 1

DIRECTIONS: Each question or incomplete statement is followed by several suggested answers or completions. Select the one that BEST answers the question or completes the statement. *PRINT THE LETTER OF THE CORRECT ANSWER IN THE SPACE AT THE RIGHT.*

1. The BEST known encyclopedia in the Western world, first published in the 18th century, was

    A. WORLD BOOK ENCYCLOPEDIA
    B. COMPTON'S PICTURED ENCYCLOPEDIA
    C. ENCYCLOPEDIA BRITANNICA
    D. ENCYCLOPEDIA AMERICANA

1.____

2. Authority-control records are important in an online catalog environment because they

    A. help prevent *blind* cross-references
    B. expand the capacity of the database
    C. keep the system from overloading
    D. provide access to fugitive materials

2.____

3. Which of the following is NOT the name of an online catalog?

    A. Geobase   B. Dynix   C. Geac   D. OCLC

3.____

4. Nom de plume is synonymous with

    A. pseudonym   B. nickname
    C. given name   D. telonism

4.____

5. Component-word searching is another way of saying _____ searching.

    A. key-word   B. permuterm
    C. subject   D. author/title

5.____

6. The citation indexes (SCIENCE CITATION INDEX, etc.) are unique in that they

    A. allow searching by the name of an institution
    B. provide access to foreign language journals
    C. allow searching of an author's references
    D. contain millions of unique records

6.____

7. A good online public access catalog (OPAC) can be expected to provide all of the following EXCEPT

    A. author and title access to books and audio-visual materials
    B. the loan status of materials that circulate
    C. information regarding who a book has been loaned to
    D. the place and publisher of each book in the catalog

7.____

8. Of the points to consider in a systematic evaluation of an encyclopedia, the LEAST important one is

    A. cost   B. viewpoint and objectivity
    C. subject coverage   D. number of pages

8.____

9. Widespread searching of bibliographic databases dates back to

   A. the 1950's B. 1960
   C. the mid-1980's D. the early 1970's

10. The format of a reference set means the

    A. writing style
    B. binding and size
    C. authority of contributors
    D. viewpoint and objectivity

11. The FIRST bibliographic databases were by-products of

    A. progress in NASA technology
    B. online card catalogs such as OCLC
    C. information dissemination centers
    D. the computerized typesetting operation

12. A patron asks your advice as a librarian on a set of encyclopedias he is considering for his family.
    The MOST helpful response for you is to

    A. give limited advice and provide the patron with professional reviews of the set under question
    B. give no advice for fear of repercussions from sales-persons and publishers
    C. endorse or condemn the set whole-heartedly, depending on your own opinion
    D. refer the patron to the director of the library

13. The four basic components of the online industry include all of the following EXCEPT

    A. libraries and information centers
    B. library school administrators
    C. end-users who request information
    D. database producers

14. McGraw-Hill's ENCYCLOPEDIA OF WORLD ART is an example of a _____ encyclopedia.

    A. children's B. subject
    C. supermarket D. foreign

15. Which of the following bibliographic databases is NOT produced by a federal government agency or federally-supported institution?

    A. ERIC B. COMPENDEX C. AGRICOLA D. MEDLINE

16. A ready-reference work is one which

    A. is allowed to circulate outside of the library
    B. is especially difficult to use
    C. arrives on a monthly basis
    D. is useful for *quick* questions of a factual nature

17. All of the following are examples of source documents EXCEPT   17.____

    A. patents   B. conference papers
    C. indexes   D. newspapers

18. The STATISTICAL ABSTRACT OF THE UNITED STATES is a compendium in the sense   18.____
    that it

    A. contains statistics on a wide range of subjects
    B. is published on an annual basis
    C. is a summary of U.S. Census data
    D. can be used for research in education

19. The number EJ121478, as part of an ERIC record, would indicate that the material referenced   19.____

    A. is a journal article
    B. is a book
    C. is an ERIC document on microfiche
    D. was entered in the database in 1978

20. A thesaurus which accompanies an index such as ERIC is a list of   20.____

    A. corporate authors   B. journals indexed
    C. stop words   D. assigned descriptors

KEY (CORRECT ANSWERS)

1.	C	11.	D
2.	A	12.	A
3.	A	13.	B
4.	A	14.	B
5.	A	15.	B
6.	C	16.	D
7.	C	17.	C
8.	D	18.	C
9.	D	19.	A
10.	B	20.	D

TEST 2

DIRECTIONS: Each question or incomplete statement is followed by several suggested answers or completions. Select the one that BEST answers the question or completes the statement. *PRINT THE LETTER OF THE CORRECT ANSWER IN THE SPACE AT THE RIGHT.*

1. The U.S. National Library of Medicine produces all of the following databases EXCEPT   1.____

   A. EMBASE   B. AIDSLINE   C. CANCERLIT   D. MEDLINE

2. H.W. Wilson's CURRENT BIOGRAPHY provides   2.____

   A. essay-length biographical information
   B. reference to information in BIOGRAPHY INDEX
   C. no more information on an individual than is provided by WHO'S WHO
   D. reviews of best-selling biographies

3. The database which provides access to fugitive materials in education is   3.____

   A. Academic Index
   B. Education Index
   C. ERIC
   D. Mental Measurements Yearbook

4. All of the following are covered in CONTEMPORARY AUTHORS EXCEPT   4.____

   A. screenwriters   B. poets
   C. dramatists   D. technical writers

5. Boolean logic utilizes all of the following logical operators EXCEPT   5.____

   A. if   B. or   C. not   D. and

6. A prescriptive dictionary is one which   6.____

   A. discusses in great detail the origin of a word
   B. adheres to tradition and historical authority for word definitions and approved usage
   C. attempts to relate every possible definition and usage of a word
   D. is published only in the United States

7. Free-text searching in a bibliographic database means   7.____

   A. searching several descriptors at one time
   B. using Boolean logic in your search
   C. searching without the use of controlled vocabulary
   D. searching only titles and abstracts

8. ABRIDGED INDEX MEDICUS differs from INDEX MEDICUS in that it   8.____

   A. contains citations to English-language journals only
   B. contains only information from the last twelve months
   C. contains citations to foreign-language journals only
   D. is not published by the National Library of Medicine

9. The two PRINCIPAL operations of public services are

    A. circulation and reference
    B. reference and serials management
    C. circulation and collection development
    D. reference and classification

10. Of the following reasons for an academic library to acquire the DICTIONARY OF AMERICAN SLANG, which is the LEAST valid?

    A. Most regular dictionaries do not indicate the variations of meaning of given slang terms or words.
    B. Students often come across expressions which are not defined well in ordinary dictionaries.
    C. It is a good source to check on the language used by an author to convey a character's background or social class.
    D. Students and librarians alike enjoy reading through it during their leisure time.

11. Collection maintenance includes all of the following EXCEPT

    A. taking inventory
    B. reshelving books
    C. identifying overdues
    D. shelf-reading

12. A gazetteer is a

    A. biographical dictionary
    B. good source for looking up phases of the moon
    C. geographical dictionary
    D. guide to motels throughout the United States

13. A Dewey Decimal Classification number never has MORE than how many digits to the LEFT of the decimal?

    A. Four   B. Five   C. Three   D. Two

14. In MOST government depository libraries, the government documents are arranged on the shelves

    A. by Superintendent of Documents numbers
    B. by Library of Congress call numbers
    C. by Dewey Decimal numbers
    D. alphabetically by title

15. The Library of Congress Classification System is different from the Dewey Decimal Classification System in that it

    A. arranges books on the shelf by subject
    B. does not include author numbers
    C. is not frequently used by libraries in the United States
    D. was developed to meet the needs of a specific library's collection

16. The BEST reference source for finding, in detail, the organization and activities of all U.S. government agencies is

    A. POLITICS IN AMERICA
    B. THE STATESMAN'S YEARBOOK
    C. UNITED STATES GOVERNMENT MANUAL
    D. MOODY'S MUNICIPAL AND GOVERNMENT MANUAL

17. The added entries in a catalog record could be for

    A. joint authors, titles, or series
    B. joint authors, series, or subjects
    C. joint authors, titles, or subjects
    D. titles, publishers, or series

18. Which of the following illustrates a directional question?

    A. How far is Syracuse from Lake Ontario?
    B. Where is the public telephone?
    C. Where can I find a biographical dictionary of presidents?
    D. Is Italy to the east of Spain?

19. You are performing an online bibliographic search for a patron and have brought up a set consisting of 300 records.
    Of the following, which is the LEAST valid way of limiting the search in order to avoid printing such a large set?

    A. Limit the search to a certain range of years
    B. Redefine the search using more specific descriptors
    C. Print only the first 40 records of the set
    D. Cut out references to articles in languages the patron cannot read

20. All of the following are examples of primary sources EXCEPT

    A. diaries   B. biographies
    C. letters   D. memoirs

21. *What is the population of Mexico City?* would MOST likely be classified as what type of reference question?

    A. Ready reference   B. Directional
    C. Research on a topic   D. Instructional

22. Something you would NOT expect to find in a vertical file is

    A. a monograph   B. a pamphlet
    C. a folded map   D. newspaper clippings

23. Logical product, logical sum, and logical difference are all part of what type of searching?

    A. Permuterm logic   B. Keyword-in-context (KWIC)
    C. Statistical logic   D. Boolean logic

24. Keyword-in-context (KWIC) indexing is also called _____ indexing.

    A. title   B. comprehensive
    C. subject   D. permutation

25. The MARC format was developed at the

    A. National Library of Medicine
    B. British Library
    C. Library of Congress
    D. Smithsonian Institute

26. Patrons of a general library are usually MOST aware of which of the following library activities?

    A. Circulation
    B. Accession
    C. Cataloging
    D. Reference

27. Three of the following four are consequences of the copyrighting of books by the U.S. government.
    Which is NOT such a consequence?

    A. Protecting author's rights
    B. Encouraging writing
    C. Securing deposit material for the government
    D. Government endorsement of the copyrighted texts

28. The term *cataloging in publication* refers to a cataloging program under which cataloging information

    A. appears in the PUBLISHERS' WEEKLY
    B. appears in the National Union Catalog
    C. appears in the publication itself
    D. is prepared by the publisher

29. The MAJOR use of a formal statement of a library's objective is

    A. serving as a guideline for program development and services
    B. justifying library staffing to the board and public
    C. convincing the governing body of the need for financial support
    D. training library staff in improved methods and practices

30. Circulation statistics should be gathered PRIMARILY for the purpose of

    A. justifying the library budget
    B. improving library service
    C. cutting library costs
    D. analyzing personnel performance

KEY (CORRECT ANSWERS)

1.	A		16.	C
2.	A		17.	A
3.	C		18.	B
4.	D		19.	C
5.	A		20.	B
6.	B		21.	A
7.	C		22.	A
8.	A		23.	D
9.	A		24.	D
10.	D		25.	C
11.	C		26.	A
12.	C		27.	D
13.	C		28.	C
14.	A		29.	A
15.	D		30.	B

TEST 3

DIRECTIONS: Each question or incomplete statement is followed by several suggested answers or completions. Select the one that BEST answers the question or completes the statement. *PRINT THE LETTER OF THE CORRECT ANSWER IN THE SPACE AT THE RIGHT.*

1. A typical reference in the READER'S GUIDE TO PERIODICAL LITERATURE would include all of the following EXCEPT   1.____

    A. author
    B. title of the article
    C. journal name
    D. journal abstract

2. An example of a subject authority list used in cataloging is the   2.____

    A. THESAURUS OF ERIC DESCRIPTORS
    B. LIBRARY OF CONGRESS SUBJECT HEADINGS
    C. NEW YORK TIMES INDEX
    D. CINAHL SUBJECT HEADING LIST

3. An example of a nonperiodical serial is   3.____

    A. EUROPA YEARBOOK
    B. AQUACULTURE MAGAZINE
    C. THE WASHINGTON POST
    D. JOURNAL OF THE AMERICAN MEDICAL ASSOCIATION

4. The Superintendent of Documents classification system arranges government documents on the shelves   4.____

    A. alphabetically by title
    B. by government agency
    C. alphabetically by author
    D. according to date of printing

5. Which of the following is an example of an open-ended question?   5.____

    A. Would you like books or magazine articles?
    B. You say you need to know the elevation of Denver?
    C. What kind of information about sharks are you looking for?
    D. Have you ever used our online catalog?

6. Scientific Information's weekly CURRENT CONTENTS consists of   6.____

    A. reproductions of journal contents pages
    B. a subject index for scientific journals
    C. author and title indexes for current periodicals
    D. scientific journal abstracts

7. All of the following are bibliographic utilities involved in resource sharing EXCEPT   7.____

    A. OCLC   B. RLIN   C. DYNIX   D. UTLAS

8. The MAIN objective of reference negotiation is to

   A. save the librarian's time
   B. steer patrons away from heavily used sources
   C. find out what the patron specifically needs
   D. instruct patrons in the proper use of reference materials

9. Which of the following PROPERLY demonstrates a logical product and logical difference search statement?

   A. Dogs and cats, not birds
   B. (Dogs or cats) and not birds
   C. Dogs and not birds or cats
   D. Dogs and (cats or birds)

10. The generally accepted definition of a serial includes all of the following EXCEPT

    A. yearbooks   B. newspapers
    C. theses   D. journals

11. ESSAY AND GENERAL LITERATURE INDEX is MOST useful for locating

    A. a specific chapter of a book
    B. magazine and journal articles
    C. biographical essays
    D. a pamphlet or newsletter

12. What do LIBRARY JOURNAL, SHEEHY'S GUIDE TO REFERENCE BOOKS, and ARBA have in common?
    They

    A. are all periodicals
    B. discuss management of online catalogs
    C. provide critical evaluation of reference materials
    D. discuss only highly recommended reference sources

13. SHORT STORY INDEX covers stories published

    A. on all subjects except science fiction
    B. in collections and the NEW YORK TIMES
    C. in collections and periodicals
    D. by American authors only

14. One way in which nonperiodical serials (such as yearbooks) are different from periodical serials (such as journals) is that nonperiodicals are

    A. published several times a year
    B. usually a collection of articles
    C. usually ordered by subscription
    D. usually acquired through a standing order

15. Of the general serial sources listed below, which is the only one that includes newspapers?

    A. STANDARD PERIODICAL DIRECTORY
    B. GALE DIRECTORY OF PUBLICATIONS
    C. ULRICH'S INTERNATIONAL PERIODICALS DIRECTORY
    D. IRREGULAR SERIALS AND ANNUALS

16. The READER'S GUIDE TO PERIODICAL LITERATURE indexes

    A. magazines and newspapers
    B. popular magazines
    C. scholarly journals
    D. short story anthologies

17. Ethnic numbers are added to classification symbols so as to arrange books by

    A. subject   B. place of printing
    C. author   D. language

18. End-matter items could include all of the following EXCEPT

    A. appendices   B. bibliographies
    C. tables of contents D. indexes

19. Which of the following BEST describes a jobber?
    A

    A. company which produces databases
    B. corporate body responsible for placing a book on the market
    C. wholesale bookseller who stocks books and supplies them to libraries
    D. person skilled in writing computer programs

20. The word *an* is a stopword on the Medline database.
    This means that

    A. it cannot be used as a search term in the database
    B. Medline includes articles such as *an* and *the* when alphabetizing by title
    C. if you type in that word, you will exit the database
    D. you cannot use Medline when searching for a title that begins with *an*

21. Of the following queries, which could NOT be answered by consulting a regular dictionary?

    A. What is the Golden Rule?
    B. How deep is a fathom?
    C. Does "humble" come from the same root as "human"?
    D. What are the rules for writing a sonnet?

22. An accurate definition of annals would be a(n)

    A. serial publication issued once a year
    B. anonymous publication
    C. record of events arranged in chronological order
    D. bibliography of an author's writings arranged by date of publication

23. West's FEDERAL PRACTICE DIGEST is an index to

   A. United States Supreme Court cases
   B. United States statutes
   C. New York State statutes
   D. The Code of Federal Regulations

24. MOST federal government documents are printed by

   A. the Government Printing Office
   B. the Library of Congress
   C. the United States Printing Office
   D. Congress

25. Setting aside a separate section for oversized books is an example of

   A. subject cataloging
   B. parallel arrangement
   C. a special materials collection
   D. Dewey Decimal Classification

KEY (CORRECT ANSWERS)

1.	D	11.	A
2.	B	12.	C
3.	A	13.	C
4.	B	14.	D
5.	C	15.	B
6.	A	16.	B
7.	C	17.	D
8.	C	18.	C
9.	A	19.	C
10.	C	20.	A

21. D
22. C
23. A
24. A
25. B

EXAMINATION SECTION
TEST 1

DIRECTIONS: Each question or incomplete statement is followed by several suggested answers or completions. Select the one that BEST answers the question or completes the statement. *PRINT THE LETTER OF THE CORRECT ANSWER IN THE SPACE AT THE RIGHT.*

1. Each of the following is a measure that is likely to be included in the usability assessment of an online catalog, EXCEPT

    A. direct observations of search behavior
    B. focus groups
    C. benchmark comparisons
    D. transaction logs

2. "Reformatting" electronic records means that

    A. they are moved from a proprietary legacy system that lacks software functionality to an open system
    B. they have been transferred from old storage media to new storage media with the same format specifications and without any loss in structure, content, or context
    C. records are exported or imported from one software environment to another without the loss of structure, content, or context even though the underlying bit stream has likely been altered
    D. there is a change to the underlying bit stream, but there is no change in the representation or intellectual content of the records

3. An accession record typically includes each of the following, EXCEPT

    A. a brief bibliographic identification
    B. the MARC record
    C. the price paid for the item
    D. the accession number

4. What is the term for the ability to move from citations in an article to those articles, and from articles to citations in a database?

    A. Click-wrap
    B. Bi-directional linking
    C. Bundling
    D. Hypertext

5. A cross-reference that would be used to direct a user from a term that is not used to a term that is used is a

    A. *see* reference
    B. *see also* reference
    C. *NOT* reference
    D. *BT* reference

6. Which of the following is a key legal issue of the Information Age?

   A. The digital divide
   B. Spam
   C. Underfunded infrastructure
   D. Copyright and fair use

7. Which of the following expenses is MOST likely to be included in a library's capital improvement budget?

   A. Library materials
   B. Salaries and wages
   C. Facilities maintenance
   D. Initial book stock

8. The archival longevity of CDs, DVDs, and videodiscs ranges from _____ years.

   A. 1-10
   B. 5-50
   C. 10-100
   D. 200-800

9. Which of the following is NOT a Web-based source of free electronic journals?

   A. Electronic Collections Online (ECO)
   B. University of Waterloo Electronic Library
   C. CIC Electronic Journals Collection
   D. New Jour archive

10. In the Dublin Core Metadata Initiative, an international effort to develop standard mechanisms for searching online resources, the _____ metadata element refers to the physical or digital manifestation of a resource.

    A. Format
    B. Type
    C. Identifier
    D. Description

11. Each of the following is typically used to increase precision in online searching, EXCEPT

    A. an "AND" operator
    B. truncation
    C. using additional concepts
    D. restricting by field

12. In _____ indexing, a human indexer or computer extracts from the title and/or text of a document one or more words or phrases to represent subject(s) of the work, for use as heading s under which entries are made.

    A. post-coordinate
    B. string
    C. derivative
    D. assignment

13. A user seeking articles about archeology should be directed to Wilson's _____ Index. 13._____

    A. Social Sciences
    B. General Science
    C. Applied Science and Technology
    D. Humanities

14. Which of the following is NOT an example of a metapublisher? 14._____

    A. High Wire
    B. MetaPress
    C. Ingenta
    D. Northern Lights

15. A "network computer" is most accurately described as a(n) 15._____

    A. computer that access and gains all of its power from a network
    B. computer that operates a network
    C. computer that can access a network
    D. network that has the functional characteristics of a computer

16. Which of the following items is MOST likely to be excluded from materials budget at a large library? 16._____

    A. Media
    B. Serials
    C. Books
    D. Electronic resources

17. Issue number 8 of a journal is identified in the MLA citation format as 17._____

    A. (8)
    B. .8
    C. No. 8
    D. :8

18. In the MARC record, which of the following fields is LEAST likely to contain an access point? 18._____

    A. 0XX
    B. 1XX
    C. 4XX
    D. 7XX

19. The user of a thesaurus of indexing terms wants to get an idea of the number of entries a search for the term is likely to retrieve. Usually, the _____ note added to the entry will provide this. 19._____

    A. scope
    B. domain
    C. postings
    D. scatter

20. William Langer's *Encyclopedia of World History* is an example of _____ arrangement.   20.___

   A. weighted
   B. topical
   C. alphabetical
   D. chronological

21. Which of the following is an example of a highly developed string-indexing system?   21.___

   A. PRECIS
   B. WordSmith
   C. MARC
   D. CiteSeer

22. In digital libraries, the methods for achieving interoperability that continue to be used most widely are ones that have moderate functionality and a low cost. Each of the following is an example, EXCEPT   22.___

   A. Z39.50
   B. HTTP
   C. URL
   D. HTML

23. In the 2001 *New York Times Co. v. Tasini* decision, the Supreme Court ruled that   23.___

   A. publishers of newspapers and periodicals infringed on the copyrights of freelance writers by making the full text of their articles publicly available in computer databases without permission
   B. Congress's passage of the Copyright Term Extension Act, which extended the duration of copyrights from life of the author plus 50 years to the life of the author plus 70 years could be applied to copyrights that existed before the law was passed
   C. the effect of the use of a copyrighted work upon the potential market for or value of the copyrighted work would be a factor that would help define whether the use is "fair" under copyright law
   D. all works for which the statutory copyright period has expires are in the public domain

24. Examples of databases include   24.___
   I. Internet search engines
   II. online library catalogs
   III. electronic periodical indexes
   IV. FirstSearch

   A. I and II
   B. II only
   C. II, III and IV
   D. I, II, III and IV

25. A major descriptor in the index entry of a bibliographic record is usually indicated by

    A. underlining
    B. italics
    C. an asterisk (*)
    D. ALL CAPS

KEY (CORRECT ANSWERS)

1. D	6. D	11. B	16. D	21. A
2. D	7. D	12. C	17. B	22. A
3. B	8. C	13. D	18. A	23. A
4. B	9. A	14. D	19. C	24. D
5. A	10. A	15. A	20. D	25. C

TEST 2

DIRECTIONS: Each question or incomplete statement is followed by several suggested answers or completions. Select the one that BEST answers the question or completes the statement. *PRINT THE LETTER OF THE CORRECT ANSWER IN THE SPACE AT THE RIGHT.*

1. A preservation administrator at a library plans to use digital imaging technology to create a digital document archive. Typically, which of the following steps in this process is performed FIRST?

    A. Image enhancement
    B. Bibliographic control
    C. Intellectual control
    D. Conversion

2. When added to HTML code, cascading style sheets

    A. allow Web site developers to automatically apply the same layout to multiple documents
    B. match source citations with target resources
    C. force a text message to pop up and replace the information content of an on-screen image
    D. allow for the running of multiple small programs within the Web-page interface

3. A user types in the term "lights" into the field of a search engine, and the results include not only "lights" but "light," "lighting," "lit," and others. The search engine offers the feature known as

    A. limits
    B. truncation
    C. stemming
    D. stop words

4. After a single copy of a one-volume work, has been acquired and processed by the library, the _____ record is attached to the full bibliographic record to track the copy.

    A. item
    B. order
    C. holdings
    D. check-in

5. Technical metadata that describe the physical characteristics of a resource are a subcategory of _____ metadata.

    A. structural
    B. digital
    C. administrative
    D. descriptive

6. A librarian is attempting to determine whether the online version of a journal is equivalent to its print counterpart. The librarian should check to see that both versions include
    I. the complete text of articles, not merely an abstract or summary
    II. letters to the editor, book reviews, feature columns, and advertisements
    III. illustrations and graphics
    IV. cross-references

    A. I and II
    B. I, II and III
    C. III and IV
    D. I, II, III and IV

6.____

7. The optimal temperature for the storage of magnetic media is around _____ degrees F.

    A. 45
    B. 55
    C. 65
    D. 75

7.____

8. The abbreviation "TOP" on a publisher's invoice usually means

    A. the requested item is nonreturnable
    B. cash is required with the order
    C. there is a new edition of the item pending
    D. the requested item is out of print for the time being

8.____

9. Pricing for a site license granted by a software vendor to a library is LEAST likely to be priced according to the

    A. terms regarding sharing and use of copies
    B. number of users in the community
    C. potential number of uses of specific content
    D. number of simultaneous users

9.____

10. Which of the following is a periodical that prints feature articles on applications of computer technologies in libraries and reviews of technology products, and which maintains a very practical focus?

    A. *Information Outlook*
    B. *Library Hi-Tech*
    C. *Computers in Libraries*
    D. *Webopedia*

10.____

11. Which of the following is a disadvantage associated with library system automation?

    A. More limited options for searching for information
    B. Increased likelihood of discouraging patrons from using the catalog
    C. Creation of additional tasks and skill sets for staff
    D. Greater difficulty in inventories and holding counts

11.____

12. Which of the following is a service that provides the online full-text of literary works in the public domain?

    A. EBSCO
    B. Northern Lights
    C. JSTOR
    D. Project Gutenberg

13. In digital libraries, many of the most recent developments in achieving interoperability are attempts to add substantial functionality at a moderate cost. Which of the following is NOT an example of this approach?

    A. XML
    B. SGML
    C. Unicode
    D. The Dublin Core

14. *http://www.lcweb.loc.gov/acq/conser/module12.html*
    In the above URL, *acq/conser* designates a

    A. filename
    B. server or hostname
    C. protocol or access scheme
    D. directory or path

15. In the Library of Congress Classification System, indexes are cataloged under

    A. LI
    B. AS
    C. IN
    D. AI

16. Which of the following periodical indexes does NOT offer full-text articles?

    A. *InfoTrac*
    B. *Readers' Guide to Periodical Literature,*
    C. *EBSCOhost*
    D. *ProQuest*

17. A scholarly journal is LEAST likely to be published

    A. weekly
    B. monthly
    C. quarterly
    D. semiannually

18. In the MLA style, items in a bibliography are arranged according to

    A. the author's surname
    B. *Library of Congress Subject Headings* classification
    C. importance
    D. title

19. A library is in the process of determining the extent of its resources. Which of the following would be identified as an "input" measure?

    A. Ratio of circulation
    B. Interlibrary loan/document delivery lending turnaround time, fill rate, and unit cost
    C. Percent of total library budget expended
    D. Number of reference questions answered

20. Which of the following MARC fields is variable in length?

    A. 001
    B. 003
    C. 005
    D. 007

21. Which of the following online databases is produced by a database vendor, rather than a subscription agent?

    A. EBSCO
    B. OCLC's Electronic Collections Online (ECO)
    C. Rowe-Com's Information Quest
    D. Blackwell Electronic Journal Navigator (EJN)

22. In a classification schedule, a _____ note instructs the cataloger to classify works in multiple locations.

    A. scope
    B. gather
    C. scatter
    D. distribution

23. Approximately what percentage of MARC fields are widely used throughout most bibliographic records?

    A. 10
    B. 30
    C. 60
    D. 90

24. The client/server model of computing, of which the Internet is the most conspicuous example, is characterized by
    I. each node or workstation having equivalent responsibilities
    II. server computers running special software that organizes and manages information
    III. individuals using client computers to access information
    IV. server computers containing the information that is accessed by users

    A. I and II
    B. I, II, and III
    C. II, III and IV
    D. I, II, III and IV

25. In most libraries, periodical issues are bound together when the issues have   25.____
    A. preserved on microform
    B. been analyzed by an indexing service
    C. fill a single shelf
    D. formed a complete volume

KEY (CORRECT ANSWERS)

1. D	6. B	11. C	16. B	21. B
2. A	7. C	12. D	17. A	22. C
3. C	8. D	13. B	18. A	23. A
4. A	9. A	14. D	19. C	24. C
5. C	10. C	15. D	20. B	25. D

EXAMINATION SECTION
TEST 1

DIRECTIONS: Each question or incomplete statement is followed by several suggested answers or completions. Select the one that BEST answers the question or completes the statement. *PRINT THE LETTER OF THE CORRECT ANSWER IN THE SPACE AT THE RIGHT.*

1. What are the two major classification systems used in American libraries to organize library materials?

    A. Dewey Decimal and Library of Congress
    B. Dewey Decimal and OCLC
    C. Library of Congress and Universal Decimal
    D. Bliss Bibliographic and Cutter Expansive

    1._____

2. The term _____ refers to creating a bibliographic record for an item using a record that has already been created by another library or organization.

    A. original cataloging
    B. archiving
    C. copy cataloging
    D. acquisitions

    2._____

3. What is the primary purpose of a call number?

    A. Educate library patrons about library classification systems
    B. Prevent theft or misplacement of library materials
    C. Provide detailed subject and description information about an item
    D. Ensure items on the same subject are placed on the same shelf in the library

    3._____

4. Which of the following would NOT be classified as a reference material?

    A. Atlas   B. Dictionary   C. Thesaurus   D. Fiction book

    4._____

5. Which library department is responsible for ordering and receiving library materials?

    A. Acquisitions   B. Circulation   C. Reference   D. IT

    5._____

6. Joni is assisting a patron who is a writer and is researching obscure information for a book. So far, Joni has been unable to find any materials at her library or other local libraries that meet the patron's needs.
Which of the following resources could Joni use to extend her search to libraries worldwide and increase her chances of locating materials for the patron?

    A. OCLC WorldCat
    B. AACR2
    C. EBSCOhost
    D. Millenium

    6._____

51

2 (#1)

7. Which of the following library materials would be classified as a serial?　　7._____

   A. Compact disc
   B. DVD
   C. Magazine
   D. Non-fiction book

8. The Dewey Decimal system divides information into _____ main classes.　　8._____

   A. 40　　　　　B. 20　　　　　C. 5　　　　　D. 10

9. Which of the following is NOT a function of OCLC?　　9._____

   A. Enabling resource sharing
   B. Providing cataloging and metadata services
   C. Managing reader's advisory services
   D. Managing digital collection services

10. _____ is the principal cataloging code used to construct bibliographic descriptions for library catalogs.　　10._____

    A. OCLC
    B. AACR2
    C. MARC
    D. Gale

Questions 11-15.

DIRECTIONS: For questions 11 through 15, match the Dewey Decimal class in Column A to the corresponding class number in Column B.

Column A	Column B	
11. Language	A. 200	11._____
12. Social sciences	B. 300	12._____
13. Literature and rhetoric	C. 400	13._____
14. Religion	D. 800	14._____
15. History and geography	E. 900	15._____

16. Which of the following is NOT a task that is typically performed by the reference department?　　16._____

    A. administering fines
    B. reader's advisory
    C. assistance with online research
    D. preparation of research guides

17. What field is marked by the 020 tag in a MARC record?

    A. Library of Congress Control Number (LCCN)
    B. Personal name main entry
    C. International Standard Book Number (ISBN)
    D. Physical description

17._____

18. The purpose of a cutter number is to organize books by

    A. subject
    B. author's last name
    C. publisher
    D. genre

18._____

19. A(n) _____ search involves using the operators AND, OR, and NOT to link keywords and concepts.

    A. reader's advisory
    B. Boolean
    C. bibliographic
    D. index

19._____

20. Chelsea works at a public library and has the primary responsibility of suggesting fiction and non-fiction books to patrons based upon their interests and needs. In her position, Chelsea is providing _____ services.

    A. interlibrary loan
    B. acquisition
    C. reader's advisory
    D. collection management

20._____

21. Which of the following databases would be most useful for helping a patron find business and legal information?

    A. ERIC
    B. Medline
    C. NoveList
    D. LexisNexis

21._____

22. A(n) _____ record is a machine readable cataloging record, which means the information in the record can be interpreted by a computer.

    A. bibliographic control
    B. MARC
    C. ILL
    D. OCLC

22._____

4 (#1)

23. A(n) _____ is a list of preferred terms used in an index or database.   23._____

    A. MARC record
    B. annotation
    C. abstract
    D. controlled vocabulary

24. What field is marked by the 100 tag in a MARC record?   24._____

    A. Title information
    B. Publication information
    C. Edition
    D. Personal name main entry

25. The first line in a Library of Congress call number is always a _____ line.   25._____

    A. whole number
    B. letter
    C. cutter
    D. date

KEY (CORRECT ANSWERS)

1. A	11. C
2. C	12. B
3. D	13. D
4. D	14. A
5. A	15. E
6. A	16. A
7. C	17. C
8. D	18. B
9. C	19. B
10. B	20. C

21. D
22. B
23. D
24. D
25. B

TEST 2

DIRECTIONS: Each question or incomplete statement is followed by several suggested answers or completions. Select the one that BEST answers the question or completes the statement. *PRINT THE LETTER OF THE CORRECT ANSWER IN THE SPACE AT THE RIGHT.*

1. The term _____ is used to refer to data about data.

   A. hypertext
   B. metadata
   C. subject heading
   D. serial

2. Which of the following storage mediums typically has the longest archival lifespan?

   A. Books
   B. Flash drives
   C. CDs
   D. Microfilm

3. In the Dewey Decimal System, what happens to class numbers as the subclass of the discipline becomes more specific?

   A. They begin to contain characters
   B. They begin to contain Roman numerals
   C. They become shorter
   D. They become longer

4. The _____ classification system consists of 1 to 3 letters followed by 1 to 4 integers.

   A. Dewey Decimal
   B. Library of Congress
   C. Bliss Bibliographic
   D. Universal Decimal

5. Which of the following is an example of a multi-subject database?

   A. LexisNexis
   B. ERIC
   C. Academic Search Premier
   D. AccessScience

6. Which of the following is NOT an example of an access point?

   A. Author   B. Title   C. Subject heading   D. Due date

7. Tamara works at a public library that uses the Dewey Decimal Classification system and she is cataloging a book about dog care. The author of the book is Karen Green. Which of the following call numbers should she assign to the book?

   A. 636.7 GRE
   B. SF 991. S6
   C. 391.5 GREEN
   D. BF 161. S4

8. _____ is a new cataloging standard based on the FRBR (functional requirements for bibliographic records) and FRAD (functional requirements for authority data) models.

   A. Resource Description and Access (RDA)
   B. OCLC Connexion
   C. Boolean logic
   D. Online Public Access Catalog (OPAC)

9. _____ maintains the largest database of bibliographic records in the world, as well as the information on which libraries own the items.

   A. Millennium   B. MARC   C. Sirius   D. OCLC

10. The term _____ refers to the items a library owns.

    A. depository   B. reserves   C. bindery   D. holdings

Questions 11-15

DIRECTIONS: In questions 11 through 15, match the Library of Congress class in Column A to the corresponding class letter in Column B.

Column A	Column B
11. Fine Arts	A. J
12. Political Science	B. L
13. Agriculture	C. N
14. Military Science	D. S
15. Education	E. U

16. In a MARC record, each field is associated with a 3-digit number called a(n) _____.

    A. serial number
    B. tag
    C. indicator
    D. ISBN

17. Which of the following is NOT a guideline for performing a reference interview? 17._____

    A. Follow-up with the patron to make sure they have everything they need
    B. Keep the patron informed of your progress as you search
    C. Ask closed-ended questions
    D. Make eye contact

18. An International Standard Bibliographic Number (ISBN) has four parts. Which of the following is NOT one of these parts? 18._____

    A. Group identifier
    B. Page count
    C. Publisher identifier
    D. Check digit

19. In a MARC record, each indicator value is _____. 19._____

    A. a number from 0 to 9
    B. a number from 10 to 20
    C. a series of non-numerical characters
    D. one lowercase letter preceded by a delimiter

20. According to the American Library Association, the term _____ refers to the right of every individual to both seek and receive information from all points of view without restriction. 20._____

    A. censorship
    B. bibliographic control
    C. resource sharing
    D. intellectual freedom

Questions 21-25.

DIRECTIONS: In questions 21 through 25, match the MARC tag in Column A to the corresponding field in Column B.

Column A	Column B	
21. 245	A. topical subject heading	21._____
22. 250	B. title information	22._____
23. 260	C. physical description	23._____
24. 300	D. edition	24._____
25. 650	E. publication information	25._____

KEY (CORRECT ANSWERS)

1. B	11. C
2. D	12. A
3. D	13. D
4. B	14. E
5. C	15. B
6. D	16. B
7. A	17. C
8. A	18. B
9. D	19. A
10. D	20. D

21. B
22. D
23. E
24. C
25. A

TEST 3

DIRECTIONS: Each question or incomplete statement is followed by several suggested answers or completions. Select the one that BEST answers the question or completes the statement. *PRINT THE LETTER OF THE CORRECT ANSWER IN THE SPACE AT THE RIGHT.*

1. Which of the following is a standard used for creating metadata?   1.____

    A. Dublin Core
    B. OCLC
    C. ERIC
    D. Boolean logic

2. A brief summary of an article is known as a(n)   2.____

    A. Database
    B. MARC record
    C. access point
    D. abstract

3. In a library, books that need repair are sent to the _____.   3.____

    A. bindery
    B. labeler
    C. wholesaler
    D. accession supervisor

4. What is the primary purpose of interlibrary loan?   4.____

    A. Increase communication between neighboring libraries
    B. Obtain materials for a patron which are not available at the patron's library
    C. Reduce the number of library materials which are damaged or missing
    D. Increase the uniformity of library cataloging records worldwide

5. Public records and historical documents would most likely be found in a library's   5.____

    A. archives
    B. serials department
    C. AV department
    D. acquisitions department

6. Which of the following is NOT a type of subject heading list?   6.____

    A. Library of Congress Subject Headings (LCSH)
    B. Sears List
    C. Cutter's Objects of the Catalog
    D. Faceted Application of Subject Terminology (FAST)

7. The term *OPAC* is often used to refer to a library's

   A. holdings
   B. classification system
   C. lending policy
   D. catalog

8. A(n) _____ is a subdivision of a more general subject heading.

   A. Index   B. abstract   C. subheading   D. holding

9. What does it mean when a library material is classified as non-circulating?

   A. The item is located in the library's archives
   B. The item can only be checked out for 24 hours
   C. The item cannot be checked out
   D. The item has not yet been cataloged

10. In a MARC record, subfield codes consist of _____.

    A. a number from 0 to 9
    B. a series of non-numerical characters
    C. a number from 10 to 20
    D. one lowercase letter, or sometimes a number, preceded by a delimiter

Questions 11-15.

DIRECTIONS: For questions 11 through 15, match the book topic in column A with the most appropriate Dewey Decimal call number in column B.

Column A	Column B
11. Bipolar disorder	A. 746.46
12. Quilting	B. 512
13. Algebra	C. 940.54
14. Hinduism	D. 616.895
15. World War II	E. 294.5

16. Linus is a cataloger at a public library, and when he catalogs he chooses subject and name headings from the Library of Congress Subject Headings list. In this example, Linus is performing

    A. authority control
    B. indexing
    C. abstracting
    D. copy cataloging

17. The purpose of an abstract is to　　　　　　　　　　　　　　　　　　　　　　　17.____

    A. summarize content
    B. provide new information
    C. sort metadata
    D. offer in depth analysis of a subject

18. If a library removes a book from its shelves because one person or group disagrees　　18.____
    with its content, this is an example of _____.

    A. intellectual freedom
    B. censorship
    C. reader's advisory
    D. plagiarism

19. Which of the following is NOT an example of a Boolean operator?　　　　　　　19.____

    A. and　　　　　B. or　　　　　C. but　　　　　D. not

20. Searching a database using "natural language" is referred to as　　　　　　　20.____

    A. Boolean logic
    B. indexing
    C. subject searching
    D. keyword searching

Questions 21-25.

DIRECTIONS: For questions 21 through 25, match the library-related term in column A with its correct meaning in column B.

Column A	Column B	
21. overdue	A. setting an item aside for a patron	21.____
22. renewal	B. an item that has not been returned by the due date	22.____
23. hold	C. a publication issued on a regular basis	23.____
24. periodical	D. section of the library containing the circulating book collection	24.____
25. stacks	E. extending the loan period of an item	25.____

KEY (CORRECT ANSWERS)

1. A
2. D
3. A
4. B
5. A

6. C
7. D
8. C
9. C
10. D

11. D
12. A
13. B
14. E
15. C

16. A
17. A
18. B
19. C
20. D

21. B
22. E
23. A
24. C
25. D

TEST 4

DIRECTIONS: Each question or incomplete statement is followed by several suggested answers or completions. Select the one that BEST answers the question or completes the statement. *PRINT THE LETTER OF THE CORRECT ANSWER IN THE SPACE AT THE RIGHT.*

1. When a library book has a size designation of quarto this indicates that its height   1._____

   A. exceeds 42 cm or its length exceeds 35 cm
   B. and length are proportionate
   C. is less than 20 cm and its length is more than 20 cm
   D. is between 29 and 42 cm, or its length is between 25 and 35 cm

2. Leah has requested a book for a patron from an out-of-state library using OCLC. The next day, while looking at the request in OCLC Request Manager, she notices that status of her request has been changed from "pending" to "conditional." What does this new status indicate about Leah's request?   2._____

   A. The lender is unwilling to send the item
   B. The lender has stated conditions for lending in the lending notes
   C. The lender has not yet viewed the request
   D. The lender has sent the item

3. When creating a call number, the cutter number is usually based on the _____, while the work mark is usually based on the _____.   3._____

   A. title; main entry
   B. publication date; main entry
   C. main entry; title
   D. title; publication date

4. Which of the following is NOT a guideline for shelving books by call number?   4._____

   A. File one decimal place at a time
   B. Ordering is based on the guideline "nothing before something"
   C. File one numerical place at a time after each capital letter
   D. File groups of letters together when they follow numbers

5. _____, which is being utilized by many libraries, refers to technologies that use radio waves to automatically identify different items.   5._____

   A. RDA   B. OCLC   C. RFID   D. WorldCat

63

6. Which of the following has no significance other than being a distinctive and definite identifier?

   A. ISBN
   B. Call number
   C. Subfield code in a MARC record
   D. ISSN

7. According to the Child Internet Protection Act (CIPA), public libraries that receive federal assistance are required to

   A. install filters on all computers
   B. visually monitor the internet use of all patrons
   C. provide separate computer stations for children
   D. deny internet access to minors

8. A(n) _____ includes its author's name, title, publisher and place of publication, and date of publication.

   A. ISSN
   B. citation to a book
   C. call number
   D. index entry

9. In which of the following scenarios would a library be infringing on copyright law?

   A. It charges a nominal fee for the use of videos
   B. It knowingly lends videos to a patron using them for a public performance
   C. It does not label videos with a copyright warning statement
   D. It sells its used videos in its annual book sale

10. An electronic version of a book that can be read on a computer or mobile device is known as a(n)

    A. e-reserve
    B. flash drive
    C. ILL
    D. e-book

11. Carol is a reference librarian and often provides reference services to patrons remotely via chat, email, instant-messaging and video conferencing. This type of reference service is known as

    A. reader's advisory
    B. proctoring
    C. virtual reference
    D. the open web

12. Thomas is a reference librarian and is trying to help a patron find a primary source about the Holocaust. Which of the following sources would be sufficient?

    A. *The Diary of Anne Frank*
    B. A biography of Adolf Hitler
    C. The film *Schindler's List*
    D. A Wikipedia entry on the Holocaust

12._____

13. When library patrons have the ability to log onto library resources like databases from an off-site location, it is known as

    A. authentication
    B. remote access
    C. virtual reference
    D. telecommuting

13._____

14. Which of the following is NOT a type of AV material?

    A. Films
    B. Slides
    C. Records
    D. Magazines

14._____

15. How do the physical descriptions of audiovisual items in MARC records differ from that of books?

    A. They are much longer
    B. They only contain alphanumeric codes
    C. They are much shorter
    D. They must be composed in complete sentences

15._____

Questions 16-20.

DIRECTIONS: For questions 16 through 20, match the OCLC interlibrary loan request status in column A with its correct meaning in column B.

Column A	Column B	
16. Received	A. the lender wants you to return the item immediately	16._____
17. In Process	B. no lender could supply the item prior to the Need Before date	17._____
18. Unfilled	C. you have already reviewed these requests	18._____
19. Expired	D. the borrower received the item from the lender	19._____
20. Recalled	E. no lender could supply the item	20._____

21. Which of the following is NOT one of the advantages of using MARC records?

    A. They allow libraries to better share bibliographic resources
    B. They prevent duplication of work
    C. They provide cataloging data that is unique and interesting
    D. They foster communication of information

22. In a MARC record, a blank, or undefined, indicator position is represented by which of the following characters?

    A. #   B. &   C. @   D. %

23. Which of the following is NOT considered a content designator in a MARC record?

    A. Tags   B. Indicators   C. Cutter numbers   D. Subfield codes

24. In a MARC record, which fields have no subfields?

    A. Only fields 001 and 002
    B. Only fields 003 and 004
    C. Fields 100 through 600
    D. Fields 001 through 009

25. A(n) _____ is a list of names, places and subjects that tells you where those names, places or subjects are discussed within a publication.

    A. biography   B. periodical   C. index   D. catalog

KEY (CORRECT ANSWERS)

1. D	11. C	21. C
2. B	12. A	22. A
3. C	13. B	23. C
4. D	14. D	24. D
5. C	15. A	25. C
6. D	16. D	
7. A	17. C	
8. B	18. E	
9. B	19. B	
10. D	20. A	

EXAMINATION SECTION
TEST 1

DIRECTIONS: Each question or incomplete statement is followed by several suggested answers or completions. Select the one that BEST answers the question or completes the statement. *PRINT THE LETTER OF THE CORRECT ANSWER IN THE SPACE AT THE RIGHT.*

1. An employee requests a book which is not in the department library.
   Of the following, the MOST advisable course of action for you to take is to

   A. attempt to get the book for him by means of the department's affiliation with the public library
   B. explain that the book is not available from the department's library
   C. suggest that he try his local public library and give him a list of local libraries
   D. tell him where he may purchase the book and offer to make the purchase for him

   1._____

2. The catalog for the use of department employees has just been thoroughly checked and revised by a professional librarian. After trying to find the name of a book in the catalog, an employee tells you that he cannot find it.
   Of the following, the MOST advisable action for you to take FIRST is to

   A. call the public library for the exact title
   B. look it up in the catalog yourself
   C. look through the stacks for the book
   D. tell him you are sorry but the book is not in the department library

   2._____

3. You find that three pages are missing from one of the copies of a very popular book in the department library.
   Of the following, the MOST advisable action for you to take is to

   A. discard the book since its usefulness is now sharply curtailed
   B. order another copy of the book but keep the old copy until the new one is received
   C. report the fact to the head of the department and request further instructions
   D. type copies of the pages from another volume of the book and tape them in the appropriate place

   3._____

4. The department library is scheduled to close at 5 P.M. It is now 4:55, and an employee reading a book shows no signs of leaving.
   Of the following, the MOST advisable action for you to take is to

   A. tell him it is time to leave
   B. tell him the time and ask him if he wishes to borrow the book
   C. turn the lights off and on, indirectly suggesting that he leave
   D. wait until he decides to leave

   4._____

5. The dealer from whom you have been buying books for the department library has informed you that henceforth he can give you only a fifteen percent instead of a twenty percent discount.
   Of the following, the MOST advisable course of action for you to take FIRST is to

   5._____

A. accept the fifteen percent discount
B. inform the head of your department
C. investigate the discount given by other book dealers
D. order directly from the publishers

6. Your supervisor is a professional librarian and is responsible for the selection of material to be added to the department library in which you are an employee. Shortly after you start on the job, an employee of the department brings you a written request to have several books of his choice added to the library.
Of the following, the MOST advisable course of action for you to take is to

    A. order the books immediately
    B. pass the suggestion along to your supervisor
    C. refuse to accept his suggestion
    D. tell him that he will have to buy the books

7. You object to your supervisor's plan to change the system in the department library from closed to open stacks.
Of the following, the MOST advisable course of action for you to take is to

    A. ask other members of the staff to support your objections
    B. await further instructions and then do as you are told
    C. discuss your objections with your supervisor
    D. send a brief report of your objections to the department head

8. Two weeks after you begin working in the department library, you learn that books in library bindings last twice as long as those with the publishers' bindings.
Of the following, the MOST advisable course of action for you to follow is to

    A. buy only paperbound books
    B. have all new books put in library bindings
    C. put in library bindings only rare editions
    D. put in library bindings only those books likely to get hard use

9. Your superior is away on an official trip. You have been asked to type and e-mail several hundred letters before he returns. Just as you begin the job, the computer breaks down.
Of the following, the MOST advisable course of action for you to take is to

    A. arrange to have the computer serviced as soon as possible
    B. write the letters by hand
    C. postpone the job until after your supervisor returns
    D. write to your supervisor for advice

10. Your supervisor in the department library is out for the day. You receive a telephone call from another city department asking if they may borrow one of the books in your library.
Of the following, the MOST advisable action for you to take FIRST is to tell the department

    A. that books are not permitted out of the department
    B. that you will check and call back the next day
    C. to send a representative to inquire the next day
    D. to write a letter to the department head

11. Two months have passed since the head of the department has borrowed one of the books in the department library. Of the following, the MOST advisable action for you to take is to

    A. ask the department head if he wishes to keep the book out longer
    B. leave a note for the department head telling him that the book should be returned immediately
    C. wait another month and then write the book off as lost
    D. wait until you receive another request for the book

12. Your supervisor tells you that he would like to have all old book cards replaced, all torn pages mended, and the books put in good condition in all other respects by the following day. You know that this is an impossible task.
    Of the following, the MOST advisable course of action for you to take is to

    A. attempt to finish as much of the job as possible
    B. explain the difficulties involved to the supervisor and await further instruction
    C. ignore the request since it is completely unreasonable
    D. make a complaint to the head of the department

13. The library in which you work has received about fifty new books. These books must be cataloged, but you have had no experience in this type of work. However, you have been told that a professional librarian will join the staff in about six weeks.
    Of the following, the MOST advisable course of action for you to take in the meantime is to

    A. close the library for a week and try to do the cataloging yourself
    B. lend the books only to those who can get special permission
    C. let the users take the books even though they are not cataloged
    D. put all the books in storage until they can be cataloged

14. The hospital library in which you work has a large back-log of books that need to be mended. You are unable to do more than a small part of the job by yourself. One of the patients in the hospital has done book binding and mending. He offers to help you because he sees the need for doing the job and because he wants something to do with his hands.
    Of the following, the MOST advisable course of action for you to take is to

    A. accept his offer on condition that the doctor approves
    B. ask him to push the book cart around the wards so you will be free to do the mending
    C. refuse his offer
    D. write a letter to his former employer to find out whether he is a good bookbinder

15. You accidentally spill a glass of water over an open book.
    Of the following, the MOST advisable action for you to take FIRST in most cases is to

    A. discard the book to prevent the water from spoiling other material
    B. hang the book up by its binding
    C. press the covers together to squeeze out the water
    D. separate the wet pages with blotters

16. In mending a book, you overturn a jar of glue on a new book.
Of the following, the MOST advisable action for you to take FIRST is to

    A. allow the glue to harden so that it may be peeled off
    B. attempt to wipe off the glue with any clean scrap paper
    C. discard the book to prevent other materials from being spoiled
    D. report the incident immediately to your supervisor

17. Of the following, the situation LEAST likely to result in injury to books is one in which

    A. all books support each other standing upright
    B. short books are placed between tall ones
    C. the books are as close together as possible
    D. the books lean against the sides of the shelves

18. Of the following, a damp cloth may BEST be used to clean a cloth book cover that has been coated with

    A. benzene   B. gold leaf
    C. turpentine D. varnish

19. Decay of leather bindings may be MOST effectively delayed by

    A. a short tanning period
    B. air conditioning
    C. rubbing periodically with a damp cloth
    D. treatment with heat

20. When paste is used to mend a page, it is MOST desirable that the page should then be

    A. aired   B. heated   C. pressed   D. sprayed

21. A book that is perfectly clean but has been used by someone with chicken pox can probably BEST be handled by

    A. burning, followed by proper disposal of the ashes
    B. forty-eight hour exposure to ultraviolet light
    C. keeping it out of circulation for six months
    D. treating it the same as any other book

22. The BEST combination of temperature and humidity for books is temperature _____ degrees, humidity _____.

    A. 50-60; 20-30%   B. 60-70; 10-20%
    C. 60-70; 50-60%   D. 70-80; 70-80%

23. When a new book is received, it is LEAST important to keep a record of the

    A. author's name
    B. cost of the book
    C. number of pages
    D. source from which it was obtained

24. You have just received from the publisher a new book for the department library, but you find that the binding is torn.
    Of the following, the MOST advisable action for you to take is to

    A. mend the binding and take no further action
    B. mend the binding but claim a price discount
    C. report the damage to the department head
    D. send the book back to the publisher

25. Of the following, a characteristic of MOST photographic charging systems is that

    A. book cards are not used
    B. charging is done by one person
    C. date due is stamped on borrower's card
    D. transaction cards are not used

KEY (CORRECT ANSWERS)

1. A
2. B
3. D
4. B
5. C
6. B
7. C
8. D
9. A
10. B

11. A
12. B
13. C
14. A
15. D
16. B
17. A
18. D
19. B
20. C

21. D
22. C
23. C
24. D
25. B

TEST 2

DIRECTIONS: Each question or incomplete statement is followed by several suggested answers or completions. Select the one that BEST answers the question or completes the statement. *PRINT THE LETTER OF THE CORRECT ANSWER IN THE SPACE AT THE RIGHT.*

1. In a card catalog, a reference from one subject heading to another is MOST commonly called a(n) _____ reference.

    A. cross   B. direct   C. primary   D. indirect

2. A book which is shortened by omission of detail but which retains the general sense of the original is called a(n)

    A. compendium   B. manuscript
    C. miniature   D. abridgment

3. An anonymous book is a

    A. book published before 1500
    B. book whose author is unknown
    C. copy which is defective
    D. work that is out of print

4. All the letters, figures, and symbols assigned to a book to indicate its location on library shelves comprise the _____ number.

    A. call   B. Cutter   C. index   D. inventory

5. The term *format* does NOT refer to a book's

    A. binding   B. size
    C. theme   D. typography

6. The term *card catalog* USUALLY refers to a

    A. catalog consisting of loose-leaf pages upon which the cards are pasted
    B. catalog in which entries are on separate cards arranged in a definite order
    C. catalog of the cards available from the Library of Congress
    D. record on cards of the works which have been weeded out of the library collection

7. The term *circulation record* USUALLY refers to a record of

    A. daily attendance
    B. the books borrowed
    C. the most popular books
    D. the books out on interlibrary loan

8. Reading shelves USUALLY involves checking the shelves to see that all the books

    A. are in the correct order
    B. are suitable for the library's patrons
    C. are there
    D. have been cataloged correctly

9. In an alphabetical catalog of book titles and authors' names, the name *de Santis* would be filed

   A. after *DeWitt*
   B. after *Sanders*
   C. before AND THEN THERE WERE NONE
   D. before *Deutsch*

10. In typing, the Shift key on the computer keyboard is used to

    A. change the font size
    B. indent a line of text
    C. type numbers
    D. type capitals

11. The abbreviation e.g. means *most nearly*

    A. as follows
    B. for example
    C. refer to
    D. that is

12. The abbreviation ff. means *most nearly*

    A. and following pages
    B. formerly
    C. frontispiece
    D. the end

13. The abbreviation ibid, means *most nearly*

    A. consult the index
    B. in the same place
    C. see below
    D. turn the page

14. *Ex libris* is a Latin phrase meaning

    A. former librarian
    B. from the books
    C. without charge
    D. without liberty

15. An expurgated edition of a book is one which

    A. contains many printing errors
    B. includes undesirable passages
    C. is not permitted in public libraries
    D. omits objectionable material

16. The re-charging of a book to a borrower is USUALLY called

    A. fining
    B. processing
    C. reissue
    D. renewal

17. A sheet of paper that is pierced with holes is

    A. borated
    B. collated
    C. perforated
    D. serrated

18. *Glossary* means *most nearly* a(n)

    A. dictionary of selected terms in a particular book or field
    B. list of chapter headings in the order in which they appear in a book
    C. section of the repairing division which coats books with a protective lacquer
    D. alphabetical table of the contents of a book

19. *Accessioning* means *most nearly*

    A. acquiring books
    B. arranging books for easy access
    C. donating books as gifts
    D. listing books in the order of purchase

20. *Bookplate* means *most nearly*

    A. a label in a book showing who owns it
    B. a metal device for holding books upright
    C. a rounded zinc surface upon which a page is printed
    D. the flat part of the binding of a book

21. *Thesaurus* means *most nearly* a book which

    A. contains instructions on how to prepare a thesis
    B. contains words grouped according to similarity of meaning
    C. describes the techniques of dramatic acting
    D. gives quotations from well-known works of literature

22. *Salacious* means *most nearly*

    A. careful   B. delicious   C. lewd   D. salty

23. *Pseudonym* means *most nearly*

    A. false report   B. fictitious name
    C. libelous statement   D. psychic phenomenon

24. *Gamut* means *most nearly* a(n)

    A. bookworm   B. simpleton
    C. vagrant   D. entire range

25. *Monograph* means *most nearly* a

    A. machine for duplicating typewritten material by means of a stencil
    B. picture reproduced on an entire page of a manuscript
    C. single chart used to represent statistical data
    D. systematic treatise on a particular subject

KEY (CORRECT ANSWERS)

1. A	11. B
2. D	12. A
3. B	13. B
4. A	14. B
5. C	15. D
6. B	16. D
7. B	17. C
8. A	18. A
9. D	19. D
10. D	20. A

21. B
22. C
23. B
24. D
25. D

TEST 3

DIRECTIONS: Each question or incomplete statement is followed by several suggested answers or completions. Select the one that BEST answers the question or completes the statement. *PRINT THE LETTER OF THE CORRECT ANSWER IN THE SPACE AT THE RIGHT.*

Questions 1-15.

DIRECTIONS: Questions 1 through 15 are to be answered SOLELY on the basis of the information contained in the following passage.

Machines may be useful for bibliographic purposes, but they will be useful only if we study the bibliographic requirements to be met and the machines available, in terms of each job which needs to be done. Many standard tools now available are more efficient than high-speed machines if the machines are used as gadgets rather than as the mechanical elements of well-considered systems.

It does not appear impossible for us to learn to think in terms of scientific management to such an extent that we may eventually be able to do much of the routine part of bibliographic work mechanically with greater efficiency, both in terms of cost per unit of service and in terms of management of the intellectual content of literature. There are many bibliographic tasks which will probably not be done mechanically in the near future because the present tools appear to present great advantages over any machine in sight; for example, author bibliography done on the electronic machines would appear to require almost as much work in instructing the machine as is required to look in an author catalog. The major field of usefulness of the machines would appear to be that of subject bibliography, and particularly in research rather than quick reference jobs.

Machines now available or in sight cannot answer a quick reference question either as fast or as economically as will consultation of standard reference works such as dictionaries, encyclopedias, or almanacs, nor would it appear worthwhile to instruct a machine and run the machine to pick out one recent book or "any recent book" in a broad subject field. It would appear, therefore, that high-speed electronic or electrical machinery may be used for bibliographic purposes only in research institutions, at least for the next five or ten years, and their use will probably be limited to research problems in those institutions. It seems quite probable that during the next decade electronic machines, including the Rapid Selector, which was designed with bibliographic purposes in mind, will find application in administrative, office, and business uses to a much greater extent than they will in bibliographic operations.

The shortcomings of machines used as gadgets have been stressed in this paper. Nevertheless, the use of machines for bibliographic purposes is developing, and it is developing rapidly. It appears quite certain that several of the machines and mechanical devices can now perform certain of the routine operations involved in bibliographic work more accurately and more efficiently than these operations can be performed without them.

At least one machine, the Rapid Selector, appears potentially capable of performing higher orders of bibliographic work than we have been able to perform in the past, if and when we learn: (a) what is really needed for the advancement of learning in the way of bibliographic services; and (b) how to utilize the machine efficiently.

There is no magic in machines as such. There will be time-lag in their application, just as there was with the typewriter. The speed and efficiency in handling the mechanical part of bibliographic work, which will determine the point of diminishing returns, depend in large measure on how long it will be before we approach these problems from the point of view of scientific management.

This report cannot solve the problem of bibliographic organization. Machines alone cannot solve the problem. We need to develop systems of handling the mass of bibliographic material, but such systems cannot be developed until we discover and establish our objectives, our plans, our standards, our methods and controls, within the framework of each situation. This may take twenty years or it may take one hundred, but it will come. The termination of how long the time-lag will be rests upon our time-lag in gathering objective information upon which scientific management of literature can be based.

1. On the basis of the above passage, machines will *probably* be MOST useful in

    A. determining the cost per unit of service
    B. quick reference jobs
    C. subject bibliography
    D. title cataloging

2. On the basis of the above passage, the Rapid Selector will *probably* be LEAST used during the next ten years in

    A. administration   B. bibliographic work
    C. business   D. office work

3. It may be inferred from the above passage that is is NOT practical to use machines to do author bibliography because

    A. experienced machine operators are not available
    B. more than one machine is needed for such a task
    C. the results obtained from a machine are unreliable
    D. too much work is involved in instructing the machine

4. On the basis of the above passage, one of the criteria of efficiency is the

    A. amount of work required   B. cost per unit of service
    C. net cost of service   D. number of machines available

5. On the basis of the above passage, the LEAST efficient of the following for quick reference jobs are

    A. bibliographies   B. dictionaries
    C. encyclopedias   D. machines

6. On the basis of the above passage, in the next few years, high-speed electronic machinery will probably be used for bibliographic purposes only by

    A. civil engineers
    B. institutions of higher education
    C. publishers
    D. research institutions

7. On the basis of the above passage, the Rapid Selector was designed for use in handling

   A. bibliographic operations
   B. computing problems
   C. photographic reproduction
   D. standard reference works

8. On the basis of the above passage, progress on the development of machines to do bibliographic tasks has reached the point at which

   A. all present tools have become obsolete
   B. certain jobs are better performed with machines than without them
   C. machines are as efficient in doing quick reference jobs as in doing special research jobs
   D. machines are no longer regarded as being too expensive

9. The one of the following which is NOT stated by the above passage to be essential in developing ways of handling bibliographic material is

   A. discovering methods and controls
   B. establishing objectives
   C. establishing standards
   D. obtaining historical data

10. The above passage indicates that machines alone will NOT be able to solve the problem of

    A. bibliographic organization
    B. reference work
    C. scientific management
    D. system analysis

11. On the basis of the above passage, the viewpoint of scientific management is essential in

    A. developing the mechanical handling of bibliographic work
    B. operating the Rapid Selector
    C. repairing electronic machines
    D. showing that people are always superior to machines in bibliographic work

12. On the basis of the above passage, there are machines in existence which

    A. are particularly useful for statistical analysis in library work
    B. are the result of scientific management of bibliographic work
    C. have not been efficiently utilized for bibliographic work
    D. may be installed in a medium-sized library

13. On the basis of the above passage, the scientific management of literature awaits the

    A. assembling of objective information
    B. compilation of new reference books
    C. development of more complex machines
    D. development of simplified machinery

14. Based on the above passage, it may be INFERRED that the author's attitude toward the use of machines in bibliographic work is that they

    A. have limited usefulness at the present time
    B. will become useful only if scientific management is applied
    C. will probably always be restricted to routine operations
    D. will probably never be useful

14.____

15. The author of the above passage believes that high-speed machines are BEST adapted to bibliographic work when they are used

    A. as gadgets
    B. in place of standard reference works
    C. to perform complex operations
    D. to perform routine operations

15.____

Questions 16-25.

DIRECTIONS: Questions 16 through 25 deal with the classification of non-fiction books according to the Dewey Classification as outlined below. For each book listed, print in the space on the right the letter in front of the class to which it belongs.

		Classification	
16.	Ernst. WORDS: ENGLISH ROOTS AND HOW THEY GROW	A. 000 General Works	16.____
17.	Faulkner. FROM VERSAILLES TO THE NEW DEAL	B. 100 Philosophy	17.____
18.	Fry. CHINESE ART	C. 200 Religion	18.____
19.	Kant. CRITIQUE OF PURE REASON	D. 300 Social Science	19.____
20.	Millikan. THE ELECTRON	E. 400 Philology	20.____
21.	Morgan. THEORY OF THE GENE	F. 500 Pure Science	21.____
22.	Raine. THE YEAR ONE; POEMS	G. 600 Applied Science, Useful Arts	22.____
23.	Richards. PRINCIPLES OF LITERARY CRITICISM	H. 700 Fine Arts	23.____
24.	Steinberg. BASIC JUDAISM	I. 800 Literature, Belleslettres	24.____
25.	Strachey. QUEEN VICTORIA	J. 900 History, Biography	25.____

KEY (CORRECT ANSWERS)

1. C
2. B
3. D
4. B
5. D

6. D
7. A
8. B
9. D
10. A

11. A
12. C
13. A
14. A
15. D

16. E
17. J
18. H
19. B
20. F

21. F
22. I
23. I
24. C
25. J

EXAMINATION SECTION
TEST 1

DIRECTIONS: Each question or incomplete statement is followed by several suggested answers or completions. Select the one that BEST answers the question or completes the statement. *PRINT THE LETTER OF THE CORRECT ANSWER IN THE SPACE AT THE RIGHT.*

1. Physical components of computers are known as 1.____
   A. software B. hardware C. firmware D. human ware

2. A touchscreen is considered a(n) _____ device. 2.____
   A. input B. output C. display D. both A and B

3. Keyboards and microphones are examples of computer 3.____
   A. peripherals B. software C. add-ons D. uploads

4. Unauthorized access to a computer is prevented through the use of 4.____
   A. passwords
   B. user logins
   C. access control software
   D. computer keys

5. In order to establish an Internet connection, a modem is always connected to a 5.____
   A. keyboard
   B. monitor
   C. telephone line
   D. printer

6. _____ does NOT hold data permanently. 6.____
   A. RAM B. ROM C. Hard drive D. Flash drive

7. Identification of a user who comes back to the same website is done through the use of 7.____
   A. scripts B. plug-in C. cookies D. both A and B

8. File _____ is the process of moving a file from one computer to another computer across the network. 8.____
   A. encryption B. transfer C. copying D. updating

9. _____ is a type of software that controls specific hardware. 9.____
   A. Driver B. Browser C. Plug-in D. Control panel

10. _____ is a downloadable program that is used for Internet surfing. 10.____
    A. Messenger B. Firefox
    C. Windows Explorer D. Internet

11. In Microsoft Word, _____ is NOT a font style. 11.____
    A. Bold B. Regular C. Superscript D. Italic

12. Which of the following is NOT associated with page margins in a Word document?
    A. Top   B. Center   C. Left   D. Right

13. Microsoft Office is a type of _____ software.
    A. application   B. system   C. Internet   D. website

14. A function that is inside another function is known as a(n) _____ function.
    A. round   B. nested   C. sum   D. average

15. To write a formula in Microsoft Excel, a user would start by typing
    A. %   B. =   C. #   D. @

16. The individual boxes used for data entry in an Excel file are known as
    A. cells
    B. data points
    C. formulas
    D. squares

17. In PowerPoint, _____ do NOT show with the slide layout.
    A. titles   B. animations C. lists   D. charts

18. _____ is a basic option when looking for colorful images or graphics to publish in a PowerPoint presentation.
    A. Clip art
    B. Online search
    C. MS Paint
    D. Drawing

19. In a web browser, the addresses of Internet pages are known as
    A. web pages   B. URLs   C. scripts   D. plug-in

20. A company that provides Internet services is called a(n)
    A. ISP   B. IBM   C. LAN   D. Both A and B

21. _____ is the process of copying a file from personal computer to a remote computer.
    A. Downloading
    B. Uploading
    C. Updating
    D. Modification

22. _____ is a text that opens another page when clicked.
    A. Link
    B. Hyperlink
    C. Both A and B
    D. Web page

23. Dots per inch is the measure of printing
    A. quality   B. type   C. time   D. layout

24. _____ is the collection of computers connected with each other.
    A. Group   B. Team   C. Network   D. Meeting

25. Which one of the following is considered a high-end printer?
    A. Dot matrix printer
    B. Inkjet printer
    C. Laser
    D. Thermal

KEY (CORRECT ANSWERS)

1. B
2. D
3. A
4. A
5. C

6. A
7. C
8. B
9. A
10. B

11. C
12. B
13. A
14. B
15. B

16. A
17. B
18. A
19. B
20. A

21. B
22. C
23. A
24. C
25. C

TEST 2

DIRECTIONS: Each question or incomplete statement is followed by several suggested answers or completions. Select the one that BEST answers the question or completes the statement. *PRINT THE LETTER OF THE CORRECT ANSWER IN THE SPACE AT THE RIGHT.*

1. Which one of the following is a storage device?   1.____
   A. Printer	B. Hard drive
   C. Scanner	D. Motherboard

2. DVD is an example of a(n) _____ disk.   2.____
   A. hard	B. optical	C. magnetic	D. floppy

3. _____ computers provide resources to other computers across the network.   3.____
   A. Server	B. Client	C. Framework	D. Digital

4. Random access memory is considered _____ computer memory.   4.____
   A. non-volatile	B. volatile	C. cache	D. permanent

5. Which one of the following is NOT an operating system?   5.____
   A. Windows	B. IOS	C. Android	D. MS Office

6. A(n) _____ is a person who gets illegal access to a computer system and steals information.   6.____
   A. administrator	B. computer operator
   C. hacker	D. programmer

7. Which one of the following is NOT application software?   7.____
   A. MS Word	B. Media player
   C. Linux	D. MS Power Point

8. Which one of the following represents a domain name?   8.____
   A. .com	B. www	C. URL	D. HTTP

9. _____ is NOT an example of an Internet browser.   9.____
   A. Opera	B. Google
   C. Mozilla	D. Internet Explorer

10. Which one of the following is/was NOT a search engine?   10.____
    A. Altavista	B. Bing
    C. Yahoo	D. Facebook

11. E-mail is an abbreviation of   11.____
    A. electronic mail	B. easy mail
    C. electric email	D. both A and B

12. A(n) _____ is a person who takes care of websites for large companies.   12.____
    A. administrator   B. webmaster
    C. programmer   D. hacker

13. _____ connect web pages with each other.   13.____
    A. Connecters   B. Links   C. Hyperlinks   D. Browsers

14. _____ is a program that is harmful for computers.   14.____
    A. Spam   B. Virus
    C. Operating system   D. Plug-in

15. CC is an abbreviation of _____ in emails.   15.____
    A. core copy   B. copycat
    C. carbon copy   D. copy copy

16. Software most commonly used for basic personal computing is   16.____
    A. Excel   B. SPSS   C. Illustrator   D. Dreamweaver

17. _____ is an option to send the same letter to different persons.   17.____
    A. Template   B. Macros   C. Mail Merge   D. Layout

18. Which one of the following is a file extension for MS Word?   18.____
    A. .doc   B. .txt   C. .bmp   D. .pdf

19. _____ displays the number of words in a document.   19.____
    A. Character Count   B. Word Count   C. Word Wrap   D. Thesaurus

20. In an Excel sheet, an active cell is specified with   20.____
    A. dotted border   B. dark wide border
    C. italic text   D. a dotted border

21. A(n) _____ is a file that contains rows and columns.   21.____
    A. database   B. spreadsheet
    C. word   D. drawing

22. _____ are objects on the slides that hold text in a PowerPoint presentation.   22.____
    A. Placeholders   B. Text holders
    C. Auto layouts   D. Object holders

23. Which one of the following brings up the first slide in a PowerPoint presentation?   23.____
    A. Ctrl+End   B. Ctrl+Home
    C. Page up   D. Next slide button

24. Which one of the following sends printing commands to a printer?   24.____
    A. F5   B. Ctrl+P   C. Ctrl+S   D. F12

25. Scanners are used to capture _____ copy of documents.   25.____
    A. soft   B. hard   C. single   D. first

KEY (CORRECT ANSWERS)

1.	B		11.	A
2.	B		12.	B
3.	A		13.	C
4.	B		14.	B
5.	D		15.	C
6.	C		16.	A
7.	C		17.	C
8.	A		18.	A
9.	B		19.	B
10.	D		20.	B

21. B
22. A
23. B
24. B
25. B

TEST 3

DIRECTIONS: Each question or incomplete statement is followed by several suggested answers or completions. Select the one that BEST answers the question or completes the statement. *PRINT THE LETTER OF THE CORRECT ANSWER IN THE SPACE AT THE RIGHT.*

1. Which one of the following is the MOST appropriate operation to move a text block in MS Word? 1.____
   A. Cut
   B. Save As
   C. Cut and Paste
   D. Copy and Paste

2. The Navigation pane opens under the _____ tab. 2.____
   A. View
   B. Review
   C. Page Layout
   D. Mailings

3. Ctrl+B makes selected test 3.____
   A. italic
   B. bold
   C. bigger
   D. uppercase

4. _____ is NOT an acceptable formula in Excel. 4.____
   A. 10+50
   B. =10+50
   C. =B7+B8
   D. =B7*B8

5. A worksheet usually contains _____ columns. 5.____
   A. 128
   B. 256
   C. 512
   D. 320

6. _____ is the process of getting data from the cell that is located in different worksheets. 6.____
   A. Accessing
   B. Referencing
   C. Updating
   D. Functioning

7. The shortcut _____ selects all PowerPoint slides at once. 7.____
   A. Ctrl+Home
   B. Ctrl+A
   C. Alt+Home
   D. Shift+A

8. By pressing Ctrl+V in a Word document, the user 8.____
   A. pastes text
   B. cuts and pastes text
   C. adds a video box
   D. deletes a page

9. Transitions are applicable only on 9.____
   A. Excel worksheets
   B. PowerPoint slides
   C. image files
   D. Word document

10. In MS Word, the _____ tab has options for margin, orientation and spacing. 10.____
    A. Design
    B. Review
    C. Page Layout
    D. Insert

11. Which one of the following is graphic software? 11.____
    A. MS Office
    B. Adobe Photoshop
    C. Firefox
    D. Notepad

12. Which one of the following is a social networking website? 12.____
    A. Facebook
    B. Yahoo
    C. Google
    D. ASK

13. A computer monitor is referred to as a(n) _____ device.
    A. output   B. input   C. sound   D. printing

14. _____ memory is another name for the main memory of the computer.
    A. Primary   B. Direct   C. Simple   D. Quick

15. An operating system is _____ software.
    A. application   B. system   C. editing   D. both A and C

16. Which one of the following pieces of equipment is necessary for video calls?
    A. Webcam   B. Mouse   C. Scanner   D. Printer

17. _____ is a primary input device that is used to enter text and numbers.
    A. Mouse   B. Keyboard   C. Joystick   D. Microphone

18. Of the following, which is NOT an example of a web browser?
    A. Firefox   B. Opera   C. Chrome   D. Google Talk

19. A _____ is a collection of many web pages that are related to each other.
    A. web browser   B. website
    C. search engine   D. Firefox

20. Which one of the following is considered a personal journal used for posts?
    A. Blog   B. E-mail   C. Chat   D. Messengers

21. Windows _____ provides security against external threats.
    A. antivirus   B. spyware   C. firmware   D. firewall

22. Desktop and laptop computers are different from each other in terms of _____ and cost.
    A. operating system   B. functions
    C. physical structure   D. application software

23. _____ is a process of stealing confidential information without permission of the user.
    A. Forwarding   B. Hacking   C. Searching   D. Complaining

24. RAM is located in the _____ board.
    A. extension   B. external   C. mother   D. chip

25. All files on the computer are stored in
    A. hard drive   B. RAM
    C. cache   D. associative memory

KEY (CORRECT ANSWERS)

1.	C	11.	B
2.	A	12.	A
3.	B	13.	A
4.	A	14.	A
5.	B	15.	B
6.	B	16.	A
7.	B	17.	B
8.	A	18.	D
9.	B	19.	B
10.	C	20.	A

21. D
22. C
23. B
24. C
25. A

TEST 4

DIRECTIONS: Each question or incomplete statement is followed by several suggested answers or completions. Select the one that BEST answers the question or completes the statement. *PRINT THE LETTER OF THE CORRECT ANSWER IN THE SPACE AT THE RIGHT.*

1. Which one of the following functions are performed by RAM? 1.____
   A. Read and Write B. Read
   C. Write D. Update

2. _____ is an example of secondary storage. 2.____
   A. Diode B. Hard disk C. RAM D. ROM

3. USB is a type of _____ storage. 3.____
   A. primary B. secondary C. tertiary D. temporary

4. MPG file extension is used for _____ files. 4.____
   A. video B. audio C. image D. flash

5. .exe is an extension for _____ files. 5.____
   A. saved B. executable C. system D. software

6. Which one of the following is NOT a type of printer? 6.____
   A. Inkjet B. Dot matrix C. Laser D. CRT

7. _____ sends digital data across a phone line. 7.____
   A. Flash B. Modem C. NIC card D. Keyboard

8. _____ is a wireless technology used to transfer data among devices over short distances. 8.____
   A. USB B. Modem C. Wi-Fi D. Bluetooth

9. A user is listening to a song on his computer's music player. He is most likely listening to a(n) _____ file. 9.____
   A. .exe B. .mus C. .wav D. .mp3

10. PNG is an extension used for _____ files. 10.____
    A. audio B. video C. text D. image

11. Cache memory is located in the 11.____
    A. monitor B. CPU C. DVD D. hard drive

12. Computer resolution determines the number of 12.____
    A. colors B. pixels C. images D. icons

13. _____ is an extension used for images. 13.____
    A. GIF B. MP3 C. MPG D. PPT

14. Which one of the following is NOT an e-mail server?
    A. Gmail   B. Yahoo   C. Chrome   D. Hotmail

15. _____ is an operating system developed by Apple.
    A. Mac IOS   B. Linux   C. Android   D. Windows

16. "What You See Is What You Get" (WYSIWYG) refers to
    A. editing text and graphics for web design
    B. buying a computer at a set price that can't be negotiated
    C. purchasing products as is on websites like Amazon and eBay
    D. printing web pages exactly as they appear on the screen

17. Which one of the following is the BEST option to add a new slide in an existing PowerPoint presentation?
    A. File, add a new slide
    B. File, open
    C. Insert, new slide
    D. File, new

18. _____ is the default setup for page orientation in PowerPoint.
    A. Horizontal   B. Vertical   C. Landscape   D. Portrait

19. Items in a list are typically shown by using
    A. graphics   B. bullets   C. icons   D. markers

20. In PowerPoint, _____ displays only text.
    A. outline view
    B. slide show
    C. print view
    D. slider sorter view

21. In Excel, a cell can be edited by use of
    A. a single click
    B. a double click
    C. the format menu
    D. formulas

22. Formulas are important features of Microsoft
    A. Word   B. PowerPoint   C. Excel   D. Publisher

23. In MS Word, which one of the following is used to underline a text?
    A. Ctrl+I   B. Ctrl+B   C. Ctrl+U   D. Ctrl+P

24. Page color option can be found under the _____ tab.
    A. Page Layout   B. Design   C. Insert   D. View

25. The F1 key typically displays a program's _____ menu.
    A. print
    B. help
    C. tools
    D. task manager

KEY (CORRECT ANSWERS)

1. A
2. B
3. C
4. A
5. B

6. D
7. B
8. D
9. D
10. D

11. B
12. B
13. A
14. C
15. A

16. A
17. C
18. C
19. B
20. A

21. A
22. C
23. C
24. B
25. B

READING COMPREHENSION
UNDERSTANDING AND INTERPRETING WRITTEN MATERIAL
EXAMINATION SECTION
TEST 1

DIRECTIONS: Each question or incomplete statement is followed by several suggested answers or completions. Select the one that BEST answers the question or completes the statement. *PRINT THE LETTER OF THE CORRECT ANSWER IN THE SPACE AT THE RIGHT.*

1. The National Assessment of Educational Progress recently released the results of the first statistically valid national sampling of young adult reading skills in the United States. According to the survey, ninety-five percent of United States young adults (aged 21-25) can read at a fourth-grade level or better. This means they can read well enough to apply for a job, understand a movie guide or join the Army. This is a higher literacy rate than the eighty to eighty-five percent usually estimated for all adults. The study also found that ninety-nine percent can write their names, eighty percent can read a map or write a check for a bill, seventy percent can understand an appliance warranty or write a letter about a billing error, twenty-five percent can calculate the amount of a tip correctly, and fewer than ten percent can correctly figure the cost of a catalog or understand a complex bus schedule.
Which statement about the study is BEST supported by the above passage?
   A. United States literacy rates among young adults are at an all-time high.
   B. Forty percent of young people in the United States cannot write a letter about a billing error.
   C. Twenty percent of United States teenagers cannot read a map,
   D. More than ninety percent of United States young adults cannot correctly calculate the cost of a catalog order.

1.____

2. It is now widely recognized that salaries, benefits, and working conditions have more of an impact on job satisfaction than on motivation. If they aren't satisfactory, work performance and morale will suffer. But even when they are high, employees will not necessarily be motivated to work well. For example, THE WALL STREET JOURNAL recently reported that as many as forty or fifty percent of newly hired Wall Street lawyers (whose salaries start at upwards of $50,000) quit within the first three years, citing long hours, pressures, and monotony as the prime offenders. It seems there's just not enough of an intellectual challenge in their jobs. An up and coming money-market executive concluded: *Whether it was $1 million or $100 million, the procedure was the same. Except for the tension, a baboon could do my job.* When money and benefits are adequate, the most important additional determinants of job satisfaction are: more responsibility, a sense of achievement, recognition, and a chance to advance. All of these factors have a more significant influence on employee motivation and performance. As a footnote, several studies have found that the absence of these non-monetary factors can lead to serious stress-related illnesses.

2.____

Which statement is BEST supported by the above passage?
  A. A worker's motivation to perform well is most affected by salaries, benefits, and working conditions.
  B. Low pay can lead to high levels of job stress.
  C. Work performance will suffer if workers feel they are not paid well.
  D. After satisfaction with pay and benefits, the next most important factor is more responsibility.

3. The establishment of joint labor-management production committees occurred in the United States during World War I and again during World War II. Their use was greatly encouraged by the National War Labor Board in World War I and the War Production Board in 1942. Because of the war, labor-management cooperation was especially desired to produce enough goods for the war effort, to reduce conflict, and to control inflation. The committees focused on how to achieve greater efficiency, and consulted on health and safety, training, absenteeism, and people issues in general. During the second world war, there were approximately five thousand labor-management committees in factories, affecting over six million workers. While research has found that only a few hundred committees made significant contributions to productivity, there were additional benefits in many cases. It became obvious to many that workers had ideas to contribute to the running of the organization, and that efficient enterprises could become even more so. Labor-management cooperation was also extended to industries that had never experienced it before. Directly after each war, however, few United States labor-management committees were in operation.
Which statement is BEST supported by the above passage?
  A. The majority of United States labor-management committees during the second world war accomplished little.
  B. A major goal of United States labor-management committees during the first and second world wars was to increase productivity.
  C. There were more United States labor-management committees during the second world war than during the first world war.
  D. There are few United States labor-management committees in operation today.

4. Studies have found that stress levels among employees who have a great deal of customer contact or a great deal of contact with the public can be very high. There are many reasons for this. Sometimes stress results when the employee is caught in the middle—an organization wants things done one way, but the customer wants them done another way. The situation becomes even worse for the employee's stress levels when he or she knows was to more effectively provide the service, but isn't allowed to, by the organization. An example is the bank teller who is required to ask a customer for two forms of identification before he or she can cash a check, even though the teller knows the customer well. If organizational mishaps occur or if there are problems with job design, the employee may be powerless to satisfy the customer, and also powerless to protect himself or herself from the customer's wrath. An example of this is the waitress who is forced to serve poorly prepared food. Studies have also found,

however, that if the organization and the employee design the positions and the service encounter well, and encourage the use of effective stress management techniques, stress can be reduced to levels that are well below average.
Which statement is BEST supported by the above passage?
- A. It is likely that knowledgeable employees will experience greater levels of job-related stress.
- B. The highest levels of occupational stress are found among those employees who have a great deal of customer contact.
- C. Organizations can contribute to the stress levels of their employees by poorly designing customer contact situations.
- D. Stress levels are generally higher in banks and restaurants.

5. It is estimated that approximately half of the United States population suffers from varying degrees of adrenal malfunction. When under stress for long periods of time, the adrenals produce extra cortisol and norepinephrine. By producing more hormones than they were designed to comfortably manufacture and secrete, the adrenals can *burn out* over time and then decrease their secretion. When this happens, the body loses its capacity to cope with stress, and the individual becomes sicker more easily and for longer periods of time. A result of adrenal malfunction may be a diminished output of cortisol. Symptoms of diminished cortisol output include any of the following: craving substances that will temporarily raise serum glucose levels such as caffeine, sweets, soda, juice, or tobacco; becoming dizzy when standing up too quickly; irritability; headaches; and erratic energy levels. Since cortisol is an anti-inflammatory hormone, a decreased output over extended periods of time can make one prone to inflammatory disease such ass arthritis, bursitis, colitis, and allergies. (Many food and pollen allergies disappear when adrenal function is restored to normal.) The patient will have no reserve energy, and infections can spread quickly. Excessive cortisol production, on the other hand, can decrease immunity, leading to frequent and prolonged illnesses.
Which statement is BEST supported by the above passage?
- A. Those who suffer from adrenal malfunction are most likely to be prone to inflammatory diseases such as arthritis and allergies.
- B. The majority of Americans suffer from varying degrees of adrenal malfunction.
- C. It is better for the health of the adrenals to drink juice instead of soda.
- D. Too much cortisol can inhibit the body's ability to resist disease.

6. Psychologist B.F. Skinner pointed out long ago that gambling is reinforced either by design or accidentally, by what he called a variable ratio schedule. A slot machine, for example, is cleverly designed to provide a payoff after it has been played a variable number of times. Although the person who plays it and wins while playing receives a great deal of monetary reinforcement, over the long run the machine will take in much more money than it pays out. Research on both animals and humans has consistently found that such variable reward schedules maintain a very high rate of repeat behavior, and that this behavior is particularly resistant to extinction.

Which statement is BEST supported by the above passage?
- A. Gambling, because it is reinforced by the variable ratio schedule, is more difficult to eliminate than most addictions.
- B. If someone is rewarded or wins consistently, even if it is not that often, he or she is likely to continue that behavior.
- C. Playing slot machines is the safest form of gambling because they are designed so that eventually the player will indeed win.
- D. A cat is likely to come when called if its owner has trained it correctly,

7. Paper entrepreneurialism is an offshoot of scientific management that has become so extreme that it has lost all connection to the actual workplace. It generates profits by cleverly manipulating rules and numbers that only in theory represent real products and real assets. At its worst, paper entrepreneurialism involves very little more than imposing losses on others for the sake of short-term profits. The others may be taxpayers, shareholders who end up indirectly subsidizing other shar holders, consumers, or investors. Paper entrepreneurialism has replaced product entrepreneurialism, is seriously threatening the United States economy, and is hurting our necessary attempts to transform the nation's industrial and productive economic base. An example is the United States company that complained loudly in 1979 that it did not have the $200 million needed to develop a video-cassette recorder, though demand for them had been very high. The company, however, did not hesitate to spend $1.2 billion that same year to buy a mediocre finance company. The video recorder market was handed over to other countries, who did not hesitate to manufacture them.

   Which statement is BEST supported by the above passage?
   - A. Paper entrepreneurialism involves very little more than imposing losses on others for the sake of short-term profits.
   - B. Shareholders are likely to benefit most from paper entrepreneurialism.
   - C. Paper entrepreneurialism is hurting the United States economy.
   - D. The United States could have made better video-cassette recorders than the Japanese but we ceded the market to them in 1979.

8. The *prisoner's dilemma* is an almost 40-year-old game-theory model psychologists, biologists, economists, and political scientists use to try to understand the dynamics of competition and cooperation. Participants in the basic version of the experiment are told that they and their *accomplice* have been caught red-handed. Together, their best strategy is to cooperate by remaining silent. If they do this, each will get off with a 30-day sentence. But either person can do better for himself or herself. If you double-cross your partner, you will go scot free while he or she serves ten years. The problem is, if you each betray the other, you will both go to prison for eight years, not thirty days. No matter what your partner chooses, you are logically better off choosing betrayal. Unfortunately, your partner realizes this too, and so the odds are good that you will both get eight years. That's the dilemma. (The length of the prison sentences is always the same for each variation.) Participants at a recent symposium on behavioral economics at Harvard University discussed the many variations on the game that have been used

over the years. In one standard version, subjects are paired with a supervisor who pays them a dollar for each point they score. Over the long run, both subjects will do best if they cooperate every time. Yet in each round, there is a great temptation to betray the other because no one knows what the other will do. The best overall strategy for this variation was found to be *tit for tat*, doing unto your opponent as he or she has just done unto you. It is a simple strategy, but very effective. The partner can easily recognize it and respond. It is retaliatory enough not to be easily exploited, but forgiving enough to allow a pattern of mutual cooperation to develop.

Which statement is BEST supported by the above passage?
- A. The best strategy for playing *prisoner's dilemma* is to cooperate and remain silent.
- B. If you double-cross your partner, and he or she does not double-cross you, your partner will receive a sentence of eight years.
- C. When playing *prisoner's dilemma*, it is best to double-cross your partner.
- D. If you double-cross your partner, and he or she double-crosses you, you will receive an eight-year sentence.

9. After many years of experience as the vice president and general manager of a large company, I feel that I know what I'm looking for in a good manager. First, the manager has to be comfortable with himself or herself, and not be arrogant or defensive. Secondly, he or she has to have a genuine interest in people. There are some managers who love ideas—and that's fine—but to be a manager, you must love people, and you must make a hobby of understanding them, believing in them and trusting them. Third, I look for a willingness and a facility to manage conflict. Gandhi defined conflict as a way of getting at the truth. Each person brings his or her own grain of truth and the conflict washes away the illusion and fantasy. Finally, a manager has to have a vision, and the ability and charisma to articulate it. A manager should be seen as a little bit crazy. Some eccentricity is an asset. People don't want to follow vanilla leaders. They want to follow chocolate-fudge-ripple leaders.

Which statement is BEST supported by the above passage?
- A. It is very important that a good manager spend time studying people.
- B. It is critical for good managers to love ideas.
- C. Managers should try to minimize or avoid conflict.
- D. Managers should be familiar with people's reactions to different flavors of ice cream.

9.____

10. Most societies maintain a certain set of values and assumptions that make their members feel either good or bad about themselves, and either better or worse than other people. In most developed countries, these values are based on the assumption that we are all free to be what we want to be, and that differences in income, work, and education are a result of our own efforts. This may make us believe that people with more income work that is more skilled, more education, and more power are somehow *better* people. We may view their achievements as proof that they have more intelligence, more motivation, and more initiative than those with lower status. The myth tells us that power, income, and education are freely and equally available to all, and that our

10.____

failure to achieve them is due to our own personal inadequacy. This simply is not the case.

The possessions we own may also seem to point to our real worth as individuals. The more we own, the more worthy of respect we may feel we are. Or, the acquisition of possessions may be a way of trying to fulfill ourselves, to make up for the loss of community and/or purpose. It is a futile pursuit because lost community and purpose can never be compensated for by better cars or fancier houses. And too often, when these things fail to satisfy, we believe it is only because we don't have enough money to buy better quality items, or more items. We feel bad that we haven't been successful enough to get all that we think we need. No matter how much we do have, goods never really satisfy for long. There is always something else to acquire, and true satisfaction eludes many, many of us.
Which statement is BEST supported by the above passage?
   A. The author would agree with the theory of *survival of the fittest*.
   B. The possessions an individual owns are not a proper measure of his or her real worth.
   C. Many countries make a sincere attempt to ensure equal access to quality education for their citizens.
   D. The effect a society's value system has on the lives of its members is greatly exaggerated.

11. *De nihilo nihil* is Latin for *nothing comes from nothing*. In the first century, the Roman poet Persius advised that if anything is to be produced of value, effort must be expended. He also said, *In nihilum nil posse revorti*—anything once produced cannot become nothing again. It is thought that Persius was parodying Lucretius, who expounded the 500-year-old physical theories of Epicurus. *De nihilo nihil* can also be used as a cynical comment, to negatively comment on something that is of poor quality produced by a person of little talent. The implication here is: *What can you expect from such a source?*
Which statement is BEST supported by the above passage?
   A. *In nihilum nil posse revorti* can be interpreted as meaning, *If anything is to be produced of value, then effort must be expended.*
   B. *De nihilo nihil* can be understood in two different ways,
   C. Lucretius was a great physicist.
   D. Persius felt that Epicurus put in little effort while developing his theories.

11.____

12. A Cornell University study has found that less than one percent of the billion pounds of pesticides used in this country annually strike their intended targets. The study found that the pesticides, which are somewhat haphazardly applied to 370 million acres, or about sixteen percent of the nation's total land area, end up polluting the environment and contaminating almost all 200,000 species of plants and animals, including humans. While the effect of indirect contamination on human cancer rates was not estimated, the study found that approximately 45,000 human pesticide poisonings occur annually, including about 3,000 cases admitted to hospitals and approximately 200 fatalities.

12.____

Which statement is BEST supported by the above passage?
   A. It is likely that indirect pesticide contamination affects human health.
   B. Pesticides are applied to over one-quarter of the total United States land area.
   C. If pesticides were applied more carefully, fewer pesticide-resistant strains of pests would develop.
   D. Human cancer rates in this country would drop considerably if pesticide use was cut in half.

13. The new conservative philosophy presents a unified, coherent approach to the world. It offers to explain much of our experience since the turbulent 1960s, and it shows what we've learned since about the dangers of indulgence and permissiveness. But it also warns that the world has become more ruthless, and that as individuals and as a nation, we must struggle for survival. It is necessary to impose responsibility and discipline in order to defeat those forces that threaten us. This lesson is dramatically clear, and can be applied to a wide range of issues.
    Which statement is BEST supported by the above passage?
    A. The 1970s were a time of permissiveness and indulgence.
    B. The new conservative philosophy may help in imposing discipline and a sense of responsibility in order to meet the difficult challenges facing this country.
    C. The world faced greater challenges during the second world war than it faces at the present time.
    D. More people identify themselves today as conservative in their political philosophy.

14. One of the most puzzling questions in management in recent years has been how usually honest, compassionate, intelligent managers can sometimes act in ways that are dishonest, uncaring, and unethical. How could top-level managers at the Manville Corporation, for example, suppress evidence for decades that proved beyond all doubt that asbestos inhalation was killing their own employees? What drove the managers of a Midwest bank to continue to act in a way that threatened to bankrupt the institution, ruin its reputation, and cost thousands of employees and investors their jobs and their savings? It's been estimated that about two out of three of America's five hundred largest corporations have been involved in some form of illegal behavior. There are, of course, some common rationalizations used to justify unethical conduct: believing that the activity is in the organization's or the individual's best interest, believing that the activity is not *really* immoral or illegal, believing that no one will ever know, or believing that the organization will sanction the behavior because it helps the organization. Ambition can distort one's sense of *duty*.
    Which statement is BEST supported by the above passage?
    A. Top-level managers of corporations are currently involved in a plan to increase ethical behavior among their employees.
    B. There are many good reasons why a manager may act unethically.
    C. Some managers allow their ambitions to override their sense of ethics,
    D. In order to successfully compete, some organizations may have to indulge in unethical or illegal behavior from time to time.

15. Some managers and supervisors believe that they are leaders because they occupy positions of responsibility and authority. But leadership is more than holding a position. It is often defined in management literature as *the ability to influence the opinions, attitudes and behaviors of others*. Obviously, there are some managers that would not qualify as leaders, and some leaders that are not *technically* managers. Research has found that many people overrate their own leadership abilities. In one recent study, seventy percent of those surveyed rated themselves in the top quartile in leadership abilities, and only two percent felt they were below average as leaders.
Which statement is BEST supported by the above passage?
   A. In a recent study, the majority of people surveyed rated themselves in the top twenty-five percent in leadership abilities.
   B. Ninety-eight percent of the people surveyed in a recent study had average or above-average leadership skills.
   C. In order to be a leader, one should hold a management position.
   D. Leadership is best defined as the ability to be liked by those one must lead.

15.____

KEY (CORRECT ANSWERS)

1.	D	6.	B	11.	B
2.	C	7.	C	12.	A
3.	B	8.	D	13.	B
4.	C	9.	A	14.	C
5.	D	10.	B	15.	A

PREPARING WRITTEN MATERIAL
EXAMINATION SECTION
TEST 1

DIRECTIONS: Each of the sentences in this test may be classified under one of the following four categories:
    A. Faulty because of incorrect grammar or word usage
    B. Faulty because of incorrect punctuation
    C. Faulty because of incorrect capitalization or incorrect spelling
    D. Correct

Examine each sentence carefully to determine under which of the above four options it is best classified. Then, in the space to the right, print the capital letter preceding the option which is the BEST of the four suggested above. (Note that each faulty sentence contains but one type of error. Consider a sentence to be correct if it contains none of the types of errors mentioned, even though there may be other correct ways of expressing the same thought.)

1. He sent the notice to the clerk who you hired yesterday.   1._____

2. It must be admitted, however that you were not informed of this change.   2._____

3. Only the employee who have served in this grade for at least two years are eligible for promotion.   3._____

4. The work was divided equally between she and Mary.   4._____

5. He thought that you were not available at that time.   5._____

6. When the messenger returns; please give him this package.   6._____

7. The new secretary prepared, typed, addressed, and delivered, the notices.   7._____

8. Walking into the room, his desk can be seen at the rear.   8._____

9. Although John has worked here longer than She, he produces a smaller amount of work.   9._____

10. She said she could of typed this report yesterday.   10._____

11. Neither one of these procedures are adequate for the efficient performance of this task.   11._____

12. The typewriter is the tool of the typist; the cash register, the tool of the cashier.   12._____

13. "The assignment must be completed as soon as possible" said the supervisor. 13._____

14. As you know, office handbooks are issued to all new Employees. 14._____

15. Writing a speech is sometimes easier than to deliver it before an audience. 15._____

16. Mr. Brown our accountant, will audit the accounts next week. 16._____

17. Give the assignment to whomever is able to do it most efficiently. 17._____

18. The supervisor expected either your or I to file these reports. 18._____

KEY (CORRECT ANSWERS)

1. A 11. A
2. B 12. C
3. D 13. B
4. A 14. C
5. D 15. A

6. B 16. B
7. B 17. A
8. A 18. A
9. C
10. A

TEST 2

DIRECTIONS: Each of the sentences in this test may be classified under one of the following four categories:
    A. Faulty because of incorrect grammar or word usage
    B. Faulty because of incorrect punctuation
    C. Faulty because of incorrect capitalization or incorrect spelling
    D. Correct

Examine each sentence carefully to determine under which of the above four options it is best classified. Then, in the space to the right, print the capital letter preceding the option which is the BEST of the four suggested above. (Note that each faulty sentence contains but one type of error. Consider a sentence to be correct if it contains none of the types of errors mentioned, even though there may be other correct ways of expressing the same thought.)

1. The fire apparently started in the storeroom, which is usually locked.   1.____

2. On approaching the victim, two bruises were noticed by this officer.   2.____

3. The officer, who was there examined the report with great care.   3.____

4. Each employee in the office had a seperate desk.   4.____

5. All employees including members of the clerical staff, were invited to the lecture.   5.____

6. The suggested Procedure is similar to the one now in use.   6.____

7. No one was more pleased with the new procedure than the chauffeur.   7.____

8. He tried to persaude her to change the procedure.   8.____

9. The total of the expenses charged to petty cash were high.   9.____

10. An understanding between him and I was finally reached.   10.____

KEY (CORRECT ANSWERS)

1.	D	6.	C
2.	A	7.	D
3.	B	8.	C
4.	C	9.	A
5.	B	10.	A

TEST 3

DIRECTIONS: Each of the sentences in this test may be classified under one of the following four categories:
- A. Faulty because of incorrect grammar or word usage
- B. Faulty because of incorrect punctuation
- C. Faulty because of incorrect capitalization or incorrect spelling
- D. Correct

Examine each sentence carefully to determine under which of the above four options it is best classified. Then, in the space to the right, print the capital letter preceding the option which is the BEST of the four suggested above. (Note that each faulty sentence contains but one type of error. Consider a sentence to be correct if it contains none of the types of errors mentioned, even though there may be other correct ways of expressing the same thought.)

1. They told both he and I that the prisoner had escaped. 1.____

2. Any superior officer, who, disregards the just complaint of his subordinates, is remiss in the performance of his duty. 2.____

3. Only those members of the national organization who resided in the Middle West attended the conference in Chicago. 3.____

4. We told him to give the national organization assignment to whoever was available. 4.____

5. Please do not disappoint and embarass us by not appearing in court. 5.____

6. Although the office's speech proved to be entertaining, the topic was not relevent to the main theme of the conference. 6.____

7. In February all new officers attended a training course in which they were learned in their principal duties and the fundamental operating procedure of the department. 7.____

8. I personally seen inmate Jones threaten inmates Smith and Green with bodily harm if they refused to participate in the plot. 8.____

9. To the layman, who on a chance visit to the prison observes everything functioning smoothly, the maintenance of prison discipline may seem to be a relatively easily realizable objective. 9.____

10. The prisoners in cell block fourty were forbidden to sit on the cell cots during the recreation hour. 10.____

KEY (CORRECT ANSWERS)

1. A   6. C
2. B   7. A
3. C   8. A
4. D   9. D
5. C   10. C

TEST 4

DIRECTIONS: Each of the sentences in this test may be classified under one of the following four categories:
- A. Faulty because of incorrect grammar or word usage
- B. Faulty because of incorrect punctuation
- C. Faulty because of incorrect capitalization or incorrect spelling
- D. Correct

Examine each sentence carefully to determine under which of the above four options it is best classified. Then, in the space to the right, print the capital letter preceding the option which is the BEST of the four suggested above. (Note that each faulty sentence contains but one type of error. Consider a sentence to be correct if it contains none of the types of errors mentioned, even though there may be other correct ways of expressing the same thought.)

1. I cannot encourage you any.
2. You always look well in those sort of clothes.
3. Shall we go to the park?
4. The man whome he introduced was Mr. Carey.
5. She saw the letter laying here this morning.
6. It should rain before the Afternoon is over.
7. They have already went home.
8. That Jackson will be elected is evident.
9. He does not hardly approve of us.
10. It was he, who won the prize.

KEY (CORRECT ANSWERS)

1. A
2. A
3. D
4. C
5. A
6. C
7. A
8. D
9. A
10. B

TEST 5

DIRECTIONS: Each of the sentences in this test may be classified under one of the following four categories:
- A. Faulty because of incorrect grammar or word usage
- B. Faulty because of incorrect punctuation
- C. Faulty because of incorrect capitalization or incorrect spelling
- D. Correct

Examine each sentence carefully to determine under which of the above four options it is best classified. Then, in the space to the right, print the capital letter preceding the option which is the BEST of the four suggested above. (Note that each faulty sentence contains but one type of error. Consider a sentence to be correct if it contains none of the types of errors mentioned, even though there may be other correct ways of expressing the same thought.)

1. Shall we go to the park.   1.____
2. They are, alike, in this particular way.   2.____
3. They gave the poor man sume food when he knocked on the door.   3.____
4. I regret the loss caused by the error.   4.____
5. The students' will have a new teacher.   5.____
6. They sweared to bring out all the facts.   6.____
7. He decided to open a branch store on 33rd street.   7.____
8. His speed is equal and more than that of a racehorse.   8.____
9. He felt very warm on that Summer day.   9.____
10. He was assisted by his friend, who lives in the next house.   10.____

KEY (CORRECT ANSWERS)

1.	B	6.	A
2.	B	7.	C
3.	C	8.	A
4.	D	9.	C
5.	B	10.	D

TEST 6

DIRECTIONS: Each of the sentences in this test may be classified under one of the following four categories:
- A. Faulty because of incorrect grammar or word usage
- B. Faulty because of incorrect punctuation
- C. Faulty because of incorrect capitalization or incorrect spelling
- D. Correct

Examine each sentence carefully to determine under which of the above four options it is best classified. Then, in the space to the right, print the capital letter preceding the option which is the BEST of the four suggested above. (Note that each faulty sentence contains but one type of error. Consider a sentence to be correct if it contains none of the types of errors mentioned, even though there may be other correct ways of expressing the same thought.)

1. The climate of New York is colder than California.   1.____
2. I shall wait for you on the corner.   2.____
3. Did we see the boy who, we think, is the leader.   3.____
4. Being a modest person, John seldom talks about his invention.   4.____
5. The gang is called the smith street bos.   5.____
6. He seen the man break into the store.   6.____
7. We expected to lay still there for quite a while.   7.____
8. He is considered to be the Leader of his organization.   8.____
9. Although I recieved an invitation, I won't go.   9.____
10. The letter must be here some place.   10.____

KEY (CORRECT ANSWERS)

1. A   6. A
2. D   7. A
3. B   8. C
4. D   9. C
5. C   10. A

TEST 7

DIRECTIONS: Each of the sentences in this test may be classified under one of the following four categories:
- A. Faulty because of incorrect grammar or word usage
- B. Faulty because of incorrect punctuation
- C. Faulty because of incorrect capitalization or incorrect spelling
- D. Correct

Examine each sentence carefully to determine under which of the above four options it is best classified. Then, in the space to the right, print the capital letter preceding the option which is the BEST of the four suggested above. (Note that each faulty sentence contains but one type of error. Consider a sentence to be correct if it contains none of the types of errors mentioned, even though there may be other correct ways of expressing the same thought.)

1. I though it to be he. 1._____
2. We expect to remain here for a long time. 2._____
3. The committee was agreed. 3._____
4. Two-thirds of the building are finished. 4._____
5. The water was froze. 5._____
6. Everyone of the salesmen must supply their own car. 6._____
7. Who is the author of Gone With the Wind? 7._____
8. He marched on and declaring that he would never surrender. 8._____
9. Who shall I say called? 9._____
10. Everyone has left but they. 10._____

KEY (CORRECT ANSWERS)

1.	A	6.	A
2.	D	7.	B
3.	D	8.	A
4.	A	9.	D
5.	A	10.	D

TEST 8

DIRECTIONS: Each of the sentences in this test may be classified under one of the following four categories:
- A. Faulty because of incorrect grammar or word usage
- B. Faulty because of incorrect punctuation
- C. Faulty because of incorrect capitalization or incorrect spelling
- D. Correct

Examine each sentence carefully to determine under which of the above four options it is best classified. Then, in the space to the right, print the capital letter preceding the option which is the BEST of the four suggested above. (Note that each faulty sentence contains but one type of error. Consider a sentence to be correct if it contains none of the types of errors mentioned, even though there may be other correct ways of expressing the same thought.)

1. Who did we give the order to?
2. Send your order in immediately.
3. I believe I paid the Bill.
4. I have not met but one person.
5. Why aren't Tom, and Fred, going to the dance?
6. What reason is there for him not going?
7. The seige of Malta was a tremendous event.
8. I was there yesterday I assure you
9. Your ukulele is better than mine.
10. No one was there only Mary.

KEY (CORRECT ANSWERS)

1. A
2. D
3. C
4. A
5. B
6. A
7. C
8. B
9. C
10. A

TEST 9

DIRECTIONS: In each of the following groups of sentences, one of the four sentences is faulty in grammar, punctuation, or capitalization. Select the INCORRECT sentence in each case.

1. A. If you had stood at home and done your homework, you would not have failed in arithmetic.
    B. Her affected manner annoyed every member of the audience.
    C. How will the new law affect our income taxes?
    D. The plants were not affected by the long, cold winter, but they succumbed to the drought of summer.

2. A. He is one of the most able men who have been in the Senate.
    B. It is he who is to blame for the lamentable mistake.
    C. Haven't you a helpful suggestion to make at this time?
    D. The money was robbed from the blind man's cup.

3. A. The amount of children in this school is steadily increasing.
    B. After taking an apple from the table, she went out to play.
    C. He borrowed a dollar from me.
    D. I had hoped my brother would arrive before me.

4. A. Whom do you think I hear from every week?
    B. Who do you think is the right man for the job?
    C. Who do you think I found in the room?
    D. He is the man whom we considered a good candidate for the presidency.

5. A. Quietly the puppy laid down before the fireplace.
    B. You have made your bed; now lie in it.
    C. I was badly sunburned because I had lain too long in the sun.
    D. I laid the doll on the bed and left the room.

KEY (CORRECT ANSWERS)

1. A
2. D
3. A
4. C
5. A

PREPARING WRITTEN MATERIAL

PARAGRAPH REARRANGEMENT
COMMENTARY

The sentences that follow are in scrambled order. You are to rearrange them in proper order and indicate the letter choice containing the correct answer at the space at the right.

Each group of sentences in this section is actually a paragraph presented in scrambled order. Each sentence in the group has a place in that paragraph; no sentence is to be left out. You are to read each group of sentences and decide upon the best order in which to put the sentences so as to form a well-organized paragraph.

The questions in this section measure the ability to solve a problem when all the facts relevant to its solution are not given.

More specifically, certain positions of responsibility and authority require the employee to discover connection between events sometimes, apparently, unrelated. In order to do this, the employee will find it necessary to correctly infer that unspecified events have probably occurred or are likely to occur. This ability becomes especially important when action must be taken on incomplete information.

Accordingly, these questions require competitors to choose among several suggested alternatives, each of which presents a different sequential arrangement of the events. Competitors must choose the MOST logical of the suggested sequences.

In order to do so, they may be required to draw on general knowledge to infer missing concepts or events that are essential to sequencing the given events. Competitors should be careful to infer only what is essential to the sequence. The plausibility of the wrong alternatives will always require the inclusion of unlikely events or of additional chains of events which are NOT essential to sequencing the given events.

It's very important to remember that you are looking for the best of the four possible choices, and that the best choice of all may not even be one of the answers you're given to choose from.

There is no one right way to solve these problems. Many people have found it helpful to first write out the order of the sentences, as they would have arranged them, on their scrap paper before looking at the possible answers. If their optimum answer is there, this can save them some time. If it isn't, this method can still give insight into solving the problem. Others find it most helpful to just go through each of the possible choices, contrasting each as they go along. You should use whatever method feels comfortable and works for you.

While most of these types of questions are not that difficult, we've added a higher percentage of the difficult type, just to give you more practice. Usually there are only one or two questions on this section that contain such subtle distinctions that you're unable to answer confidently. And you then may find yourself stuck deciding between two possible choices, neither of which you're sure about.

EXAMINATION SECTION
TEST 1

DIRECTIONS: The following groups of sentences need to be arranged in an order that makes sense. Select the letter preceding the sequence that represents the BEST sentence order. *PRINT THE LETTER OF THE CORRECT ANSWER IN THE SPACE AT THE RIGHT.*

1.
   I. The keyboard was purposely designed to be a little awkward to slow typists down.
   II. The arrangement of letters on the keyboard of a typewriter was not designed for the convenience of the typist.
   III. Fortunately, no one is suggesting that a new keyboard be designed right away.
   IV. If one were, we would have to learn to type all over again.
   V. The reason was that the early machines were slower than the typists and would jam easily.
   The CORRECT answer is:
   A. I, III, IV, II, V
   B. II, V, I, IV, III
   C. V, I, II, III, IV
   D. II, I, V, III, IV

2.
   I. The majority of the new service jobs are part-time or low-paying.
   II. According to the U.S. Bureau of Labor Statistics, jobs in the service sector constitute 72% of all jobs in this country.
   III. If more and more workers receive less and less money, who will buy the goods and services needed to keep the economy going?
   IV. The service sector is by far the fastest growing part of the United States economy.
   V. Some economists look upon this trend with great concern.
   The CORRECT answer is:
   A. II, IV, I, V, III
   B. II, III, IV, I, V
   C. V, IV, II, III, I
   D. III, I, II, IV, V

3.
   I. They can also affect one's endurance.
   II. This can stabilize blood sugar levels, and ensure that the brain is receiving a steady, constant, supply of glucose, so that one is *hitting on all cylinders* while taking the test.
   III. By food, we mean real food, not junk food or unhealthy snacks.
   IV. For this reason, it is important not to skip a meal, and to bring food with you to the exam.
   V. One's blood sugar levels can affect how clearly one is able to think and concentrate during an exam.
   The CORRECT answer is:
   A. V, IV, II, III, I
   B. V, II, I, IV, III
   C. V, I, IV, III, II
   D. V, IV, I, III, II

1.____

2.____

3.____

4. I. Those who are the embodiment of desire are absorbed in material quests, and those who are the embodiment of feeling are warriors who value power more than possession.
    II. These qualities are in everyone, but in different degrees.
    III. But those who value understanding yearn not for goods or victory, but for knowledge.
    IV. According to Plato, human behavior flows from three main sources: desire, emotion, and knowledge.
    V. In the perfect state, the industrial forces would produce but not rule, the military would protect but not rule, and the forces of knowledge, the philosopher kings, would reign.
    The CORRECT answer is:
    A. IV, V, I, II, III
    B. V, I, II, III, IV
    C. IV, III, II, I, V
    D. IV, II, I, III, V

5. I. Of the more than 26,000 tons of garbage produced daily in New York City, 12,000 tons arrive daily at Fresh Kills.
    II. In a month, enough garbage accumulates there to fill the Empire State Building.
    III. In 1937, the Supreme Court halted the practice of dumping the trash of New York City into the sea.
    IV. Although the garbage is compacted, in a few years the mounds of garbage at Fresh Kills will be the highest points south of Maine's Mount Desert Island on the Eastern Seaboard.
    V. Instead, tugboats now pull barges of much of the trash to Staten Island and the largest landfill in the world, Fresh Kills.
    The CORRECT answer is:
    A. III, V, IV, I, II
    B. III, V, II, IV, I
    C. III, V, I, II, IV
    D. III, II, V, IV, I

6. I. Communists rank equality very high, but freedom very low.
    II. Unlike communists, conservatives place a high value on freedom and a very low value on equality.
    III. A recent study demonstrated that one way to classify people's political beliefs is to look at the importance placed on two words: freedom and equality.
    IV. Thus, by demonstrating how members of these groups feel about the two words, the study has proved to be useful for political analysts in several European countries.
    V. According to the study, socialists and liberals rank both freedom and equality very high, while fascists rate both very low.
    The CORRECT answer is:
    A. III, V, I, II, IV
    B. V, IV, III, I, II
    C. III, V, IV, II, I
    D. III, I, II, IV, V

7.
   I. "Can there be anything more amazing than this?"
   II. If the riddle is successfully answered, his dead brothers will be brought back to life.
   III. "Even though man sees those around him dying every day," says Dharmaraj, "he still believes and acts as if he were immortal."
   IV. "What is the cause of ceaseless wonder?" asks the Lord of the Lake.
   V. In the ancient epic, The Mahabharata, a riddle is asked of one of the Pandava brothers.
   The CORRECT answer is:
   A. V, II, I, IV, III
   B. V, IV, III, I, II
   C. V, II, IV, III, I
   D. V, II, IV, I, III

8.
   I. On the contrary, the two main theories—the cooperative (neoclassical) theory and the radical (labor theory)—clearly rest on very different assumptions, which have very different ethical overtones.
   II. The distribution of income is the primary factor in determining the relative levels of material well-being that different groups or individuals attain.
   III. Of all issues in economics, the distribution of income is one of the most controversial.
   IV. The neoclassical theory tends to support the existing income distribution (or minor changes), while the labor theory ends to support substantial changes in the way income is distributed.
   V. The intensity of the controversy reflects the fact that different economic theories are not purely neutral, *detached* theories with no ethical or moral implications.
   The CORRECT answer is:
   A. II, I, V, IV, III
   B. III, II, V, I, IV
   C. III, V, II, I, IV
   D. III, V, IV, I, II

9.
   I. The pool acts as a broker and ensures that the cheapest power gets used first.
   II. Every six seconds, the pool's computer monitors all of the generating stations in the state and decides which to ask for more power and which to cut back.
   III. The buying and selling of electrical power is handled by the New York Power Pool in Guilderland, New York.
   IV. This is to the advantage of both the buying and selling utilities.
   V. The pool began operation in 1970, and consists of the state's eight electric utilities.
   The CORRECT answer is:
   A. V, I, II, III, IV
   B. IV, II, I, III, V
   C. III, V, I, IV, II
   D. V, III, IV, II, I

10.
   I. Modern English is much simpler grammatically than Old English.
   II. Finnish grammar is very complicated; there are some fifteen cases, for example.
   III. Chinese, a very old language, may seem to be the exception, but it is the great number of characters/words that must be mastered that makes it so difficult to learn, not its grammar.
   IV. The newest literary language—that is, written as well as spoken—is Finish, whose literary roots go back only to about the middle of the nineteenth century.
   V. Contrary to popular belief, the longer a language is been in use the simpler its grammar—not the reverse.

   The CORRECT answer is:
   A. IV, I, II, III, V
   B. V, I, IV, II, III
   C. I, II, IV, III, V
   D. IV, II, III, I, V

10._____

KEY (CORRECT ANSWERS)

1.	D	6.	A
2.	A	7.	C
3.	C	8.	B
4.	D	9.	C
5.	C	10.	B

TEST 2

DIRECTIONS: This type of question tests your ability to recognize accurate paraphrasing, well-constructed paragraphs, and appropriate style and tone. It is important that the answer you select contains only the facts or concepts given in the original sentences. It is also important that you be aware of incomplete sentences, inappropriate transitions, unsupported opinions, incorrect usage, and illogical sentence order. Paragraphs that do not include all the necessary facts and concepts, that distort them, or that add new ones are not considered correct.

The format for this section may vary. Sometimes, long paragraphs are given, and emphasis is placed on style and organization. Our first five questions are of this type. Other times, the paragraphs are shorter, and there is less emphasis on style and more emphasis on accurate representation of information. Our second group of five questions are of this nature.

For each of Questions 1 through 10, select the paragraph that BEST expresses the ideas contained in the sentences above it. *PRINT THE LETTER OF THE CORRECT ANSWER IN THE SPACE AT THE RIGHT.*

1. I. Listening skills are very important for managers.
    II. Listening skills are not usually emphasized.
    III. Whenever managers are depicted in books, manuals or the media, they are always talking, never listening.
    IV. We'd like you to read the enclosed handout on listening skills and to try to consciously apply them this week.
    V. We guarantee they will improve the quality of your interactions.

    A. Unfortunately, listening skills are not usually emphasized for managers. Managers are always depicted as talking, never listening. We'd like you to read the enclosed handout on listening skills. Please try to apply these principles this week. If you do, we guarantee they will improve the quality of your interactions.
    B. The enclosed handout on listening skills will be important improving the quality of your interactions. We guarantee it. All you have to do is take sometime this week to read and to consciously try to apply the principles. Listening skills are very important for manages, but they are not usually emphasized. Whenever managers are depicted in books, manuals or the media, they are always talking, never listening.
    C. Listening well is one of the most important skills a manager can have, yet it's not usually given much attention. Think about any representation of managers in books, manuals, or in the media that you may have seen. They're always talking, never listening. We'd like you to read the enclosed handout on listening skills and consciously try to apply them the rest of the week. We guarantee you will see a difference in the quality of your interactions.

1.____

D. Effective listening, one very important tool in the effective manager's arsenal, is usually not emphasized enough. The usual depiction of managers in books, manuals or the media is one in which they are always talking, never listening. We'd like you to read the enclosed handout and consciously try to apply the information contained therein throughout the rest of the week. We feel sure that you will see a marked difference in the quality of your interactions.

2. I. Chekhov wrote three dramatic masterpieces which share certain themes and formats: <u>Uncle Vanya</u>, <u>The Cherry Orchard</u>, and <u>The Three Sisters</u>.
    II. They are primarily concerned with the passage of time and how this erodes human aspirations.
    III. The plays are haunted by the ghosts of the wasted life.
    IV. The characters are concerned with life's lesser problems; however, such as the inability to make decisions, loyalty to the wrong cause, and the inability to be clear.
    V. This results in sweet, almost aching, type of a sadness referred to as Chekhovian.

    2.____

    A. Chekhov wrote three dramatic masterpieces: <u>Uncle Vanya</u>, <u>The Cherry Orchard</u>, and <u>The Three Sisters</u>. These masterpieces share certain themes and formats: the passage of time, how time erodes human aspirations, and the ghosts of wasted life. Each masterpiece is characterized by a sweet, almost aching, type of sadness that has become known as Chekhovian. The sweetness of this sadness hinges on the fact that it is not the great tragedies of life which are destroying these characters, but their minor flaws: indecisiveness, misplaced loyalty, unclarity.
    B. <u>The Cherry Orchard</u>, <u>Uncle Vanya</u>, and <u>The Three Sisters</u> are three dramatic masterpieces written by Chekhov that use similar formats to explore a common theme. Each is primarily concerned with the way that passing time wears down human aspirations, and each is haunted by the ghosts of the wasted life. The characters are shown struggling futilely with the lesser problems of life: indecisiveness, loyalty to the wrong cause, and the inability to be clear. These struggles create a mood of sweet, almost aching, sadness that has become known as Chekhovian.
    C. Chekhov's dramatic masterpieces are, along with <u>The Cherry Orchard</u>, <u>Uncle Vanya</u>, and <u>The Three Sisters</u>. These plays share certain thematic and formal similarities. They are concerned most of all with the passage of time and the way in which time erodes human aspirations. Each play is haunted by the specter of the wasted life. Chekhov's characters are caught, however, by life's lesser snares: indecisiveness, loyalty to the wrong cause, and unclarity. The characteristic mood is a sweet, almost aching type of sadness that has come to be known as Chekhovian.
    D. A Chekhovian mood is characterized by sweet, almost aching, sadness. The term comes from three dramatic tragedies by Chekhov which revolve around the sadness of a wasted life. The three masterpieces (<u>Uncle Vanya</u>, <u>The Three Sisters</u>, and <u>The Cherry Orchard</u>) share the same

theme and format. The plays are concerned with how the passage of time erodes human aspirations. They are peopled with characters who are struggling with life's lesser problems. These are people who are indecisive, loyal to the wrong causes, or are unable to make themselves clear.

3.
I. Movie previews have often helped producers decide which parts of movies they should take out or leave in.
II. The first 1933 preview of King Kong was very helpful to the producers because many people ran screaming from the theater and would not return when four men first attacked by Kong were eaten by giant spiders.
III. The 1950 premiere of Sunset Boulevard resulted in the filming of an entirely new beginning, and a delay of six months in the film's release.
IV. In the original opening scene, William Holden was in a morgue talking with thirty-six other "corpses" about the ways some of them had died.
V. When he began to tell them of his life with Gloria Swanson, the audience found this hilarious, instead of taking the scene seriously.

3._____

A. Movie previews have often helped producers decide what parts of movies they should leave in or take out. For example, the first preview of King Kong in 1933 was very helpful. In one scene, four men were first attacked by Kong and then eaten by giant spiders. Many members of the audience ran screaming from the theater and would not return. The premiere of the 1950 film Sunset Boulevard was also very helpful. In the original opening scene, William Holden was in a morgue with thirty-six other "corpses," discussing the ways some of them had died. When he began to tell them of his life with Gloria Swanson, the audience found this hilarious. They were supposed to take the scene seriously. The result was a delay of six months in the release of the film while a new beginning was added.

B. Movie previews have often helped producers decide whether they should change various parts of a movie. After the 1933 preview of King Kong, a scene in which four men who had been attacked by Kong were eaten by giant spiders was taken out as many people ran screaming from the theater and would not return. The 1950 premiere of Sunset Boulevard also led to some changes. In the original opening scene, William Holden was in a morgue talking with thirty-six other "corpses" about the ways some of them had died. When he began to tell them of his life with Gloria Swanson, the audience found this hilarious, instead of taking the scene seriously.

C. What do Sunset Boulevard and King Kong have in common? Both show the value of using movie previews to test audience reaction. The first 1933 preview of King Kong showed that a scene showing four men being eaten by giant spiders after having been attacked by Kong was too frightening for many people. They ran screaming from the theater and couldn't be coaxed back. The 1950 premiere of Sunset Boulevard was also a scream, but not the kind the producers intended. The movie opens with William Holden lying in a morgue discussing the ways they had died with thirty-six other "corpses." When he began to tell them of his life with Gloria Swanson, the audience couldn't take him seriously. Their laughter caused a six-month delay while the beginning was rewritten.

D. Producers very often use movie previews to decide if changes are needed. The premiere of Sunset Boulevard in 1950 led to a new beginning and a six-month delay in film release. At the beginning, William Holden and thirty-six other "corpses" discuss the ways some of them died. Rather than taking this seriously, the audience thought it was hilarious when he began to tell them of his life with Gloria Swanson. The first 1933 preview of King Kong was very helpful for its producers because one scene so terrified the audience that many of them ran screaming from the theater and would not return. In this particular scene, four men who had first been attacked by Kong were eaten by giant spiders.

4. I. It is common for supervisors to view employees as "things" to be manipulated.   4.____
    II. This approach does not motivate employees, nor does the carrot-and-stick approach because employees often recognize these behaviors and resent them.
    III. Supervisors can change these behaviors by using self-inquiry and persistence.
    IV. The best managers genuinely respect those they work with, are supportive and helpful, and are interested in working as a team with those they supervise.
    V. They disagree with the Golden Rule that says "he or she who has the gold makes the rules."

    A. Some managers act as if they think the Golden Rule means "he or she who has the gold makes the rules." They show disrespect to employees by seeing them as "things" to be manipulated. Obviously, this approach does not motivate employees any more than the carrot-and-stick approach motivates them. The employees are smart enough to spot these behaviors and resent them. On the other hand, the managers genuinely respect those they work with, are supportive and helpful, and are interested in working as a team. Self-inquiry and persistence can change even the former type of supervisor into the latter.
    B. Many supervisors all into the trap of viewing employees as "things" to be manipulated, or try to motivate them by using a carrot-and-stick approach. These methods do not motivate employees, who often recognize the behaviors and resent them. Supervisors can change these behaviors, however, by using self-inquiry and persistence. The best managers are supportive and helpful, and have genuine respect for those with whom they work. They are interested in working as a team with those they supervise. To them, the Golden Rule is not "he or she who has the gold makes the rules."
    C. Some supervisors see employees as "things" to be used or manipulated using a carrot-and-stick technique. These methods don't work. Employees often see through them and resent them. A supervisor who

wants to change may do so. The techniques of self-inquiry and persistence can be used to turn him or her into the type of supervisor who doesn't think the Golden Rule is "he or she who has the gold makes the rules." They may become like the best managers who treat those with whom they work with respect and give them help and support. These are the manager who know how to build a team.

D. Unfortunately, many supervisors act as if their employees are objects whose movements they can position at will. This mistaken belief has the same result as another popular motivational technique—the carrot-and-stick approach. Both attitudes can lead to the same result—resentment from those employees who recognize the behaviors for what they are. Supervisors who recognize these behaviors can change through the use of persistence and the use of self-inquiry. It's important to remember that the best managers respect their employees. They readily give necessary help and support and are interested in working as a team with those they supervise. To these managers, the Golden Rule is not "he or she who has the gold makes the rules."

5.
I. The first half of the nineteenth century produced a group of pessimistic poets—Byron, De Musset, Heine, Pushkin, and Leopardi.
II. It also produced a group of pessimistic composers—Schubert, Chopin, Schumann, and even the later Beethoven.
III. Above all, in philosophy, there was the profoundly pessimistic philosopher, Schopenhauer.
IV. The Revolution was dead, the Bourbons were restored, the feudal barons were reclaiming their land, and progress everywhere was being suppressed, as the great age was over.
V. "I thank God," said Goethe, "that I am not young in so thoroughly finished a world."

5._____

A. "I thank God," said Goethe, "that I am not young in so thoroughly finished a world." The Revolution was dead, the Bourbons were restored, the feudal barons were reclaiming their land, and progress everywhere was being suppressed. The first half of the nineteenth century produced a group of pessimistic poets: Byron, De Musset, Heine, Pushkin, and Leopardi. It also produced pessimistic composers: Schubert, Chopin, Schumann. Although Beethoven came later, he fits into this group, too. Finally and above all, it also produced a profoundly pessimistic philosopher, Schopenhauer. The great age was over.

B. The first half of the nineteenth century produced a group of pessimistic poets: Byron, De Musset, Heine, Pushkin, and Leopardi. It produced a group of pessimistic composers: Schubert, Chopin, Schumann, and even the later Beethoven. Above all, it produced a profoundly pessimistic philosopher, Schopenhauer. For each of these men, the great age was over. The Revolution was dead, and the Bourbons were restored. The feudal barons were reclaiming their land, and progress everywhere was being suppressed.

C. The great age was over. The Revolution was dead—the Bourbons were restored, and the feudal barons were reclaiming their land. Progress everywhere was being suppressed. Out of this climate came a profound pessimism. Poets, like Byron, De Musset, Heine, Pushkin, and Leopardi; composers, like Schubert, Chopin, Schumann, and even the later Beethoven; and above all, a profoundly pessimistic philosopher, Schopenauer. This pessimism which arose in the first half of the nineteenth century is illustrated by these words of Goethe, "I thank God that I am not young in so thoroughly finished a world."

D. The first half of the nineteenth century produced a group of pessimistic poets, Byron, De Musset, Heine, Pushkin, and Leopardi—and a group of pessimistic composers, Schubert, Chopin, Schumann, and the later Beethoven. Above it all, it produced a profoundly pessimistic philosopher, Schopenhauer. The great age was over. The Revolution was dead, the Bourbons were restored, the feudal barons were reclaiming their land, and progress everywhere was being suppressed. "I thank God," said Goethe, "that I am not young in so thoroughly finished a world."

6. I. A new manager sometimes may feel insecure about his or her competence in the new position.
   II. The new manager may then exhibit defensive or arrogant behavior towards those one supervises, or the new manager may direct overly flattering behavior toward one's new supervisor.

   A. Sometimes, a new manager may feel insecure about his or her ability to perform well in this new position. The insecurity may lead him or her to treat others differently. He or she may display arrogant or defensive behavior towards those he or she supervises, or be overly flattering to his or her new supervisor.
   B. A new manager may sometimes feel insecure about his or her ability to perform well in the new position. He or she may then become arrogant, defensive, or overly flattering towards those he or she works with.
   C. There are times when a new manager may be insecure about how well he or she can perform in the new job. The new manager may also behave defensive or act in an arrogant way towards those he or she supervises, or overly flatter his or her boss.
   D. Sometimes a new manager may feel insecure about his or her ability to perform well in the new position. He or she may then display arrogant or defensive behavior towards those they supervise, or become overly flattering towards their supervisors.

6._____

7. I. It is possible to eliminate unwanted behavior by bringing it under stimulus control—tying the behavior to a cue, and then never, or rarely, giving the cue.
   II. One trainer successfully used this method to keep an energetic young porpoise from coming out of her tank whenever she felt like it, which was potentially dangerous.
   III. Her trainer taught her to do it for a reward, in response to a hand signal, and then rarely gave the signal.

7._____

A. Unwanted behavior can be eliminated by tying the behavior to a cue, and then never, or rarely, giving the cue. This is called stimulus control. One trainer was able to use this method to keep an energetic young porpoise from coming out of her tank by teaching her to come out for a reward in response to a hand signal, and then rarely giving the signal.

B. Stimulus control can be used to eliminate unwanted behavior. In this method, behavior is tied to a cue, and then the cue is rarely, if ever, given. One trainer was able to successfully use stimulus control to keep an energetic young porpoise from coming out of her tank whenever she felt like it—a potentially dangerous practice. She taught the porpoise to come out for a reward when she gave a hand signal, and then rarely gave the signal.

C. It is possible to eliminate behavior that is undesirable by bringing it under stimulus control by tying behavior to a signal, and then rarely giving the signal. One trainer successfully used this method to keep an energetic porpoise from coming out of her tank, a potentially dangerous situation. Her trainer taught the porpoise to do it for a reward, in response to a hand signal, and then would rarely give the signal.

D. By using stimulus control, it is possible to eliminate unwanted behavior by tying the behavior to a cue, and then rarely or never give the cue. One trainer was able to use this method to successfully stop a young porpoise from coming out of her tank whenever she felt like it. To curb this potentially dangerous practice, the porpoise was taught by the trainer to come out of the tank for a reward, in response to a hand signal, and then rarely given the signal.

8. I. There is a great deal of concern over the safety of commercial trucks, caused by their greatly increased role in serious accidents since federal deregulation in 1981.
   II. Recently, 60 percent of trucks in New York and Connecticut and 70 percent of trucks in Maryland randomly stopped by state troopers failed safety inspections.
   III. Sixteen states in the United States require no training at all for truck drivers.

   A. Since federal deregulation in 1981, there has been a great deal of concern over the safety of commercial trucks, and their greatly increased role in serious accidents. Recently, 60 percent of trucks in New York and Connecticut, and 70 percent of trucks in Maryland failed safety inspections. Sixteen states in the United States require no training at all for truck drivers.

   B. There is a great deal of concern over the safety of commercial trucks since federal deregulation in 1981. Their role in serious accidents has greatly increased. Recently, 60 percent of trucks randomly stopped in Connecticut and New York and 70 percent in Maryland failed safety inspections conducted by state troopers. Sixteen states in the United States provide no training at all for truck drivers.

   C. Commercial trucks have a greatly increased role in serious accidents since federal deregulation in 1981. This has led to a great deal of concern.

8._____

Recently, 70 percent of trucks in Maryland and 60 percent of trucks in New York and Connecticut failed inspection of those that were randomly stopped by state troopers. Sixteen states in the United States require no training for all truck drivers.

D. Since federal deregulation in 1981, the role that commercial trucks have played in serious accidents has greatly increased, and this has led to a great deal of concern. Recently, 60 percent of trucks in New York and Connecticut, and 70 percent of trucks in Maryland randomly stopped by state troopers failed safety inspections. Sixteen states in the U.S. don't require any training for truck drivers.

9.
I. No matter how much some people have, they still feel unsatisfied and want more, or want to keep what they have forever.
II. One recent television documentary showed several people flying from New York to Paris for a one-day shopping spree to buy platinum earrings, because they were bored.
III. In Brazil, some people were ordering coffins that cost a minimum of $45,000 and are equipping them with deluxe stereos, televisions, and other graveyard necessities.

9.____

A. Some people, despite having a great deal, still feel unsatisfied and want more, or think they can keep what they have forever. One recent documentary on television showed several people enroute from Paris to New York for a one day shopping spree to buy platinum earrings, because they were bored. Some people in Brazil are even ordering coffins equipped with such graveyard necessities as deluxe stereos and televisions. The price of the coffins start at $45,000.
B. No matter how much some people have, they may feel unsatisfied. This leads them to want more, or to want to keep what they have forever. Recently, a television documentary depicting several people flying from New York to Paris for a one day shopping spree to buy platinum earrings. They were bored. Some people in Brazil are ordering coffins that cost at least $45,000 and come equipped with deluxe televisions, stereos and other necessary graveyard items.
C. Some people will be dissatisfied no matter how much they have. They may want more, or they may want to keep what they have forever. One recent television documentary showed several people, motivated by boredom, jetting from New York to Paris for a one-day shopping spree to buy platinum earrings. In Brazil, some people are ordering coffins equipped with deluxe stereos, televisions and other graveyard necessities. The minimum price for these coffins—$45,000.
D. Some people are never satisfied. No matter how much they have they still want more, or think they can keep what they have forever. One television documentary recently showed several people flying from New York to Paris for the day to buy platinum earrings because they were bored. In Brazil, some people are ordering coffins that cost $45,000 and are equipped with deluxe stereos, televisions and other graveyard necessities.

10. I. A television signal or video signal has three parts.
    II. Its parts are the black-and-white portion, the color portion, and the synchronizing (sync) pulses, which keep the picture stable.
    III. Each video source, whether it's a camera or a video-cassette recorder contains its own generator of these synchronizing pulses to accompany the picture that it's sending in order to keep it steady and straight.
    IV. In order to produce a clean recording, a video-cassette recorder must "lock-up" to the sync pulses that are part of the video it is trying to record, and this effort may be very noticeable if the device does not have gunlock.

    A. There are three parts to a television or video signal: the black-and-white part, the color part, and the synchronizing (sync) pulses, which keep the picture stable. Whether it's a video-cassette recorder or a camera, each video source contains its own pulse that synchronizes and generates the picture it's sending in order to keep it straight and steady. A video-cassette recorder must "lock up" to the sync pulses that are part of the video it's trying to record. If the device doesn't have gunlock, this effort must be very noticeable.
    B. A video signal or television is comprised of three parts: the black-and-white portion, the color portion, and the sync (synchronizing) pulses, which keep the picture stable. Whether it's a camera or a video-cassette recorder, each video source contains its own generator of these synchronizing pulses. These accompany the picture that it's sending in order to keep it straight and steady. A video-cassette recorder must "lock up" to the sync pulses that are part of the video it is trying to record in order to produce a clean recording. This effort may be very noticeable if the device does not have gunlock.
    C. There are three parts to a television or video signal: the color portion, the black-and-white portion, and the sync (synchronizing pulses). These keep the picture stable. Each video source, whether it's a video-cassette recorder or a camera, generates these synchronizing pulses accompanying the picture it's sending in order to keep it straight and steady. If a clean recording is to be produced, a video-cassette recorder must store the sync pulses that are part of the video it is trying to record. This effort may not be noticeable if the device does not have gunlock.
    D. A television signal or video signal has three parts: the black-and-white portion, the color portion, and the synchronizing (sync) pulses. It's the sync pulses which keep the picture stable, which accompany it and keep it steady and straight. Whether it's a camera or a video-cassette recorder, each video source contains its own generator of these synchronizing pulses. To produce a clean recording, a video-cassette recorder must "lock up" to the sync pulses that are part of the video it is trying to record. If the device does not have gunlock, this effort may be very noticeable.

KEY (CORRECT ANSWERS)

1. C
2. B
3. A
4. B
5. D

6. A
7. B
8. D
9. C
10. D

INTERPRETING STATISTICAL DATA GRAPHS, CHARTS, AND TABLES

EXAMINATION SECTION

TEST 1

DIRECTIONS: Each question or incomplete statement is followed by several suggested answers or completions. Select the one that BEST answers the question or completes the statement. *PRINT THE LETTER OF THE CORRECT ANSWER IN THE SPACE AT THE RIGHT.*

Questions 1-12.

DIRECTIONS: Questions 1 through 12 are to be answered SOLELY on the basis of the information given in the graph and chart below.

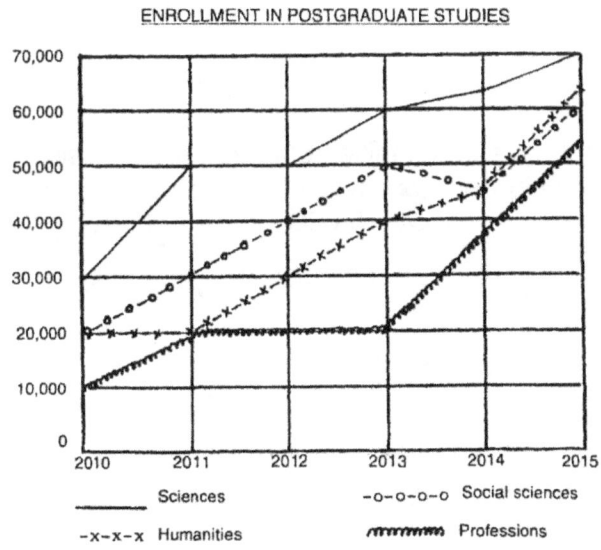

ENROLLMENT IN POSTGRADUATE STUDIES

——— Sciences -o-o-o-o- Social sciences
-x-x-x- Humanities ⁄⁄⁄⁄⁄⁄⁄⁄ Professions

Fields	Subdivisions	2014	2015
Sciences	Math	10,000	12,000
	Physical Science	22,000	24,000
	Behavioral Science	32,000	35,000
Humanities	Literature	26,000	34,000
	Philosophy	6,000	8,000
	Religion	4,000	6,000
	Arts	10,000	16,000
Social Services	History	36,000	46,000
	Sociology	8,000	14,000
Professions	Law	2,000	2,000
	Medicine	6,000	8,000
	Business	30,000	44,000

2 (#1)

1. The number of students enrolled in the social sciences and in the humanities was the same in
   A. 2012 and 2014
   B. 2010 and 2014
   C. 2014 and 2015
   D. 2011 and 2014

   1._____

2. A comparison of the enrollment of students in the various postgraduate studies shows that in every year from 2010 through 2015, there were MORE students enrolled in _____ than in the _____.
   A. professions; sciences
   B. humanities; professions
   C. social sciences, professions
   D. humanities; sciences

   2._____

3. The number of students enrolled in the humanities was GREATER than the number of students enrolled in the professions by the same amount in _____ of the years.
   A. two
   B. three
   C. four
   D. five

   3._____

4. The one field of postgraduate study to show a DECREASE in enrollment in one year compared to the year immediately preceding is
   A. humanities
   B. sciences
   C. professions
   D. social sciences

   4._____

5. If the proportion of arts students to all humanities students was the same in 2012 as in 2015, then the number of arts students in 2012 was
   A. 7,500
   B. 13,000
   C. 15,000
   D. 5,000

   5._____

6. In which field of postgraduate study did enrollment INCREASE by 20 percent from 2012 to 2013?
   A. Humanities
   B. Professions
   C. Sciences
   D. Social sciences

   6._____

7. The GREATEST increase in overall enrollment took place between
   A. 2010 and 2011
   B. 2012 and 2013
   C. 2013 and 2014
   D. 2013 and 2015

   7._____

8. Between 2012 and 2015, the combined enrollment of the sciences and social sciences INCREASED by
   A. 40,000
   B. 48,000
   C. 50,000
   D. 54,000

   8._____

9. If the enrollment in the social sciences had decreased from 2014 to 2015 at the same rate as from 2013 to 2014, then the social science enrollment in 2015 would have differed from the humanities enrollment in 2015 MOST NEARLY by
   A. 6,000
   B. 8,000
   C. 12,000
   D. 22,000

   9._____

10. In the humanities, the GREATEST percentage increase in enrollment from 2014 to 2015 was in
    A. literature
    B. philosophy
    C. religion
    D. arts

    10._____

11. If the proportion of behavioral science students to the total number of students in the sciences was the same in 2011 as in 2014, then the increase in behavioral science enrollment from 2011 to 2015 was
    A. 5,000　　　B. 7,000　　　C. 10,000　　　D. 14,000

12. If enrollment in the professions increased at the same rate from 2015 to 2016 as from 2014 to 2015, the enrollment in the professions in 2001 would be MOST NEARLY
    A. 85,000　　　B. 75,000　　　C. 60,000　　　D. 55,000

KEY (CORRECT ANSWERS)

1.	B	7.	D
2.	C	8.	A
3.	B	9.	D
4.	D	10.	D
5.	A	11.	C
6.	C	12.	B

TEST 2

DIRECTIONS: Each question or incomplete statement is followed by several suggested answers or completions. Select the one that BEST answers the question or completes the statement. *PRINT THE LETTER OF THE CORRECT ANSWER IN THE SPACE AT THE RIGHT.*

Questions 1-5.

DIRECTIONS: Questions 1 through 5 involve calculations of annual grade averages for college students who have just completed their junior year. These averages are to be based on the following table showing the number of credit hours for each student during the year at each of the grade levels: A, B, C, D, and F. How these letter grades may be translated into numerical grades is indicated in the first column of the table.

Grade Value	Credit Hours – Junior Year					
	King	Lewis	Martin	Nonkin	Ottly	Perry
A = 95	12	23	9	15	6	3
B = 85	9	12	9	12	18	6
C = 75	6	6	9	3	3	21
D = 65	3	3	3	3	-	-
F = 0	-	-	3	-	-	-

Calculating a grade average for an individual student is a four-step process:
  I. Multiply each grade value by the number of credit hours for which the student received that grade.
  II. Add these multiplication products for each student.
  III. Add the student's total credit hours.
  IV. Divide the multiplication product total by the total number of credit hours.
  V. Round the result, if there is a decimal place, to the nearest whole number. A number ending in .5 would be rounded to the next higher number.

EXAMPLE:

Using student King's grades as an example, his grade average can be calculated by going through the following four steps:

  I. $95 \times 12 = 1140$
  II. $85 \times 9 = 765$
  III. $75 \times 6 = 450$
  IV. $65 \times 3 = 195$
  V. $0 \times 0 = 0$

  II. TOTAL = 2550

  III. 12
       9
       6
       3
       0
  30 TOTAL CREDIT HOURS

  IV. Divide 2550 by 30: $\frac{2550}{30} = 85$.

King's grade average is 85.

1. The grade average of Lewis is
   A. 83   B. 84   C. 85   D. 86

2 (#2)

2. The grade average of Martin is
   A. 72 B. 73 C. 74 D. 75

3. The grade average of Nonkin is
   A. 85 B. 86 C. 87 D. 88

4. Student Ottly must attain a grade average of 90 in each of his years in college to be accepted into the graduate school of his choice.
   If, in summer school during his junior year, he takes two three-credit courses and receives a grade of 95 in each one, his grade average for his junior year will then be MOST NEARLY
   A. 87 B. 88 C. 89 D. 90

5. If Perry takes an additional three-credit course during the year and receives a grade of 95, his grade average will be increased to APPROXIMATELY
   A. 79 B. 80 C. 81 D. 82

KEY (CORRECT ANSWERS)

1. C
2. D
3. C
4. B
5. B

TEST 3

DIRECTIONS: Each question or incomplete statement is followed by several suggested answers or completions. Select the one that BEST answers the question or completes the statement. *PRINT THE LETTER OF THE CORRECT ANSWER IN THE SPACE AT THE RIGHT.*

Questions 1-5.

DIRECTIONS: Questions 1 through 5 are to be answered SOLELY on the basis of the following information and chart.

The following table gives pertinent data for six different applicants with regard to: Grade averages, which are expressed on a scale running from 0 (low) to 4 (high); Scores on qualifying test, which run from 200 (low) to 800 (high); Related work experience, which is expressed in number of months; Personal references, which are related from 1 (low) to 5 (high).

Applicant	Grade Average	Test Score	Work Experience	Reference
Jones	2.2	620	24	3
Perez	3.5	650	0	5
Lowitz	3.2	420	2	4
Uncker	2.1	710	15	2
Farrow	2.8	560	0	3
Shapiro	3.0	560	12	4

An administrative Assistant is in charge of the initial screening process for the program. This process requires classifying applicants into the following four groups:

A. SUPERIOR CANDIDATES: Unless the personal reference rating is lower than 3, all applicants with grade averages of 3.0 or higher and test scores of 600 or higher are classified as superior candidates.

B. GOOD CANDIDATES: Unless the personal reference rating is lower than 3, all applicants with one of the following combinations of grade averages and test scores are classified as good candidates:
   1. Grade average of 2.5 to 2.9 and test score of 600 or higher;
   2. Grade average of 3.0 or higher and test score of 550 to 599.

C. POSSIBLE CANDIDATES: Applicants with one of the following combinations of qualifications are classified as possible candidates:
   1. Grade average of 2.5 to 2.9 and test score of 550 to 599 and a personal reference rating of 3 or higher;
   2. Grade average of 2.0 to 2.4 and test score of 500 or higher and at least 21 months' work experience and a personal reference rating of 3 or higher;
   3. A combination of grade average and test score that would otherwise qualify as superior or good but a personal reference score lower than 3.

D. REJECTED CANDIDATES: Applicants who do not fall in any of the above groups are to be rejected.

EXAMPLE:
Jones' grade average of 2.2 does not meet the standard for either a superior candidate (grade average must be 3.0 or higher) or a good candidate (grade average must be 2.5 to 2.9). Grade average of 2.2 does not qualify Jones as a possible candidate if Jones has a test score of 500 or higher, at least 21 months' work experience, and a personal reference rating of 3 or higher. Since Jones has a test score of 620, 24 months' work experience, and a reference rating of 3, Jones is a possible candidate. The answer is C.

Answer Questions 1 through 5 as explained above, indicating for each whether the applicant should be classified as a
    A. Superior candidate   B. Good candidate
    C. Possible candidate   D. Rejected candidate

1. Perez
2. Lowitz
3. Uncker
4. Farrow
5. Shapiro

KEY (CORRECT ANSWERS)

1. A
2. D
3. D
4. C
5. B

BASIC FUNDAMENTALS OF LIBRARY SCIENCE

TABLE OF CONTENTS

	Page
DEWEY DECIMAL SYSTEM	1
PREPARING TO USE THE LIBRARY	1
THREE TYPES OF BOOK CARDS	2
Author Card	2
Title Card	2
Subject Card	3
Call Number	3
PERIODICALS	3
PERIODICALS FILE	3
PERIODICAL INDEXES	3
TEST IN LIBRARY SCIENCE	4
I. Using a Card Catalog	4
II. Understanding Entries in a Periodical Index	5
III. Identifying Library Terms	7
IV. Finding a Book by its Call Number	7
V. General	9
KEY (CORRECT ANSWERS)	10

BASIC FUNDAMENTALS OF LIBRARY SCIENCE

The problem of classifying' all human knowledge has produced a branch of learning called "library science." A lasting contribution to a simple and understandable method of locating a book on any topic was designed by Melvil Dewey in 1876. His plan divided all knowledge into ten large classes and then dubdivided each class according to related groups.

DEWEY DECIMAL SYSTEM

1. Subject Classification

The Dewey Decimal Classification System is the accepted and most widely used subject classification system in libraries throughout the world.

2. Classification by Three (3) Groups

There are three groups of classification in the system. A basic group of ten (10) classifications arranges all knowledge as represented by books within groups by classifications numbered 000-900.

The second group is the "100 division"; each group of the basic "10 divisions" is again divided into 9 sub-sctions allowing for more detailed and specialized subjects not identified in the 10 basic divisions.

3. There is a third, still further specialized "One thousand" group where each of the "100" classifications are further divided by decimalized, more specified, subject classifications. The "1,000" group is mainly used by highly specialized scientific and much diversified libraries.

These are the subject classes of the Dewey System:

000-099	General works (included bibliography, encyclopedias, collections, periodicals, newspapers,etc.)
100-199	Philosophy (includes psychology, logic, ethics, conduct, etc.) 200-299 Religion (includes mythology, natural theology, Bible, church history, etc.)
300-399	Social Science (includes economics, government, law, education, commerce, etc.)
400-499	Language (includes dictionaries, grammars, philology, etc.) 500-599 Science (includes mathematics, chemistry, physics, astronomy, geology, etc.) 600-699 Useful Arts (includes agriculture, engineering, aviation, medicine, manufactures, etc.) 700-799 Fine Arts (includes sculpture, painting, music, photography, gardening, etc.)
800-899	Literature (includes poetry, plays, orations, etc.) 900-999 History (includes geoegraphy, travel, biography, ancient and modern history, etc.)

PREPARING TO USE THE LIBRARY

Your ability to use the library and its resources is an important factor in determining your success. Skill and efficiency in finding the library materials you need for assignments and research papers will increase the amount of time you have to devote to reading or organizing information.

These are some of the preparations you can make now.
1. Develop skill in using your local library. You can increase your familiarity with the card catalog and the periodical indexes, such as the *Readers' Guide to Periodical Literature,* in any library.
2. Take the *Test in Library Science* to see how you can improve your knowledge of the library.
3. Read in such books as *Books, Libraries and You* by Jessie Edna Boyd, *The Library Key* by Margaret G. Cook, and *Making Books Work, a Guide to the Use of Libraries* by Jennie Maas Flexner.

You can find other titles by looking under the subject heading LIBRARIES AND READERS in the card catalog of your library. THREE TYPES OF BOOK CARDS

Here are the three general types of cards which are used to represent a book in the main catalog.

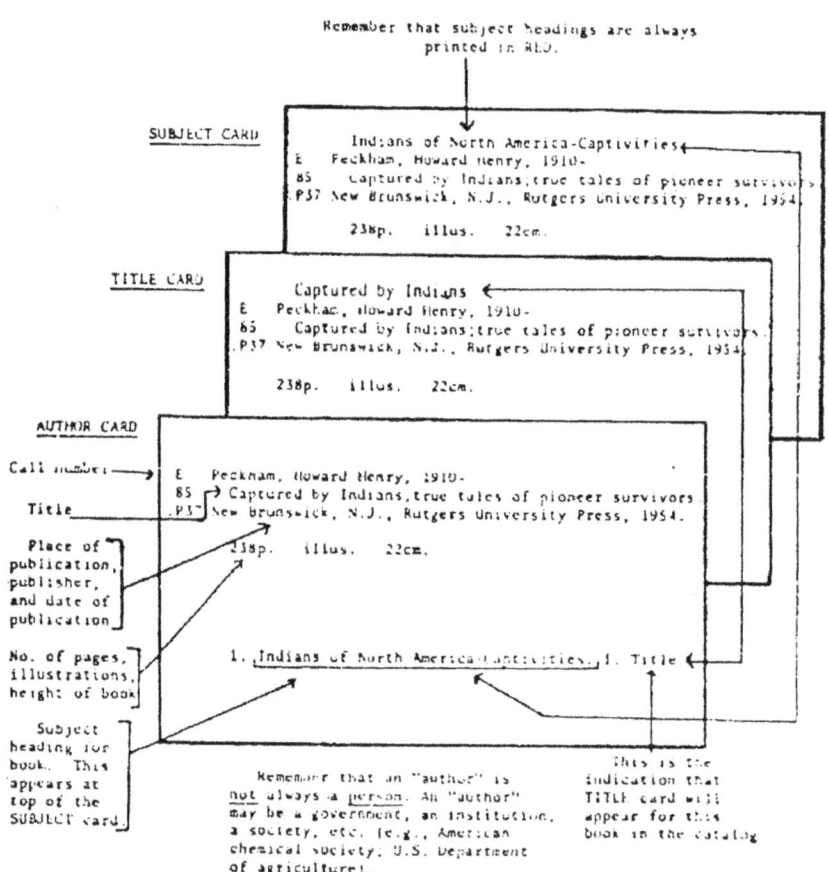

CARD CATALOG

The Card Catalog lists all books in the library by author. The majority of books also have title and subject cards.

Author card

If the author is known, look in the catalog under the author's name. The "author" for some works may be a society, an institution, or a government department.

Title card

Books with distinctive titles, anonymous works and periodicals will have a title card.

Subject card

To find books on a specific subject, look in the catalog under that subject heading. (Subject headings are printed in red on the Catalog Card.)

Call number

The letters and numbers in the upper left-hand corner *of the* Catalog Card are the book's call number. Copy this call number accurately, for it will determine the shelf location of the book. The word "Reference" marked in red in the upper right-hand corner of the catalog card indicates that the item is shelved in the Reference Section, and "Periodical "marked in yellow on the Catalog Card indicates that the item is shelved in the Periodicals Section. PERIODICALS

All magazines are arranged in alphabetical order by title. PERIODICALS FILE

To determine whether the Library has a specific magazine, consult the Periodicals File. Check the title of the magazine needed, and note that there are two cards for each title.

The bottom card lists the current issues available. The top card lists back bound volumes.

Those marked "Ask at Ref.Desk" may be obtained from the Reference Librarian. PERIODICAL INDEXES

Material in magazines is more up-to-date than books and is a valuable source of information. To find articles on a chosen subject, use the periodical indexes.

The Readers' Guide to Periodical Literature is the most familiar of these indexes. In the front of each volume is a list of the periodicals indexed and a key to abbreviations. Similar aids appear in the front of other periodical indexes.

Sample entry: WEASELS

   WONDERFUL WHITE WEASEL. R.Beck. il OUTDOOR LIFE 135:48-9+ Ja '65

Explanation :   An illustrated article on the subject WEASELS entitled WONDERFUL WHITE WEASEL, by R.Beck, will be found in volume 135 of OUTDOOR LIFE, pages 48-9 (continued on later pages of the same issue), the January 1965 number.

Major libraries subscribe to the following indexes:
Art Index
Biography Index
Book Review Index
British Humanities Index
Essay and General Literature Index
   This is helpful for locating criticism of works of literature.
An Index to Book Reviews in the Humanities
International Index ceased publications June, 1965 and continued as Social Science and
   Humanities Index
The Music Index The New York
Times Index Nineteenth Century Readers' Guide
Poole's Index
Poverty and Human Resources Abstracts
Psychological Abstracts
Public Affairs Information Service.Bulletin of the (PAIS) is a subject index to current
   books,pamphlets,periodical articles, government documents, and other library materials
   in economics and public affairs.

4

<u>Readers' Guide to Periodical Literature</u>
<u>Social Science and Humanities Index a continuation of the International Index</u>
<u>Sociological Abstracts</u>

Do you have the basic skills for using a library efficiently? You should be able to answer AT LEAST 33 of the following questions correctly. *CHECK YOUR ANSWERS BY TURNING TO THE ANSWER KEY AT THE BACK OF THIS SECTION.*
USING A CARD CATALOG
Questions 1-9.

DIRECTIONS: An author card (or "main entry" card) is shown below. Identify each item on the card by selecting the CORRECT letters for them. *PRINT THE LETTER OF THE CORRECT ANSWER IN THE SPACE AT THE RIGHT.*

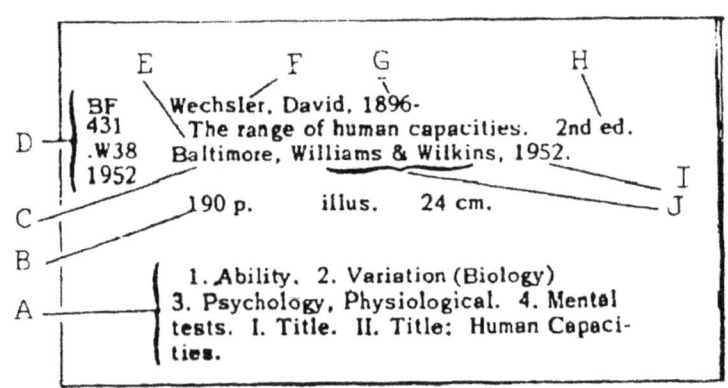

Sample Answer:

0.   <u>F</u>

1. Date book was published. 1.___

2. Number of pages in book. 2.___

3. Title. 3.___

4. Place of publication. 4.___

5. Call number. 5.___

6. Year author was born 6.___

7. Edition. 7.___

8. Publisher. 8.___

9. Other headings under which cards for this book may be found. 9.___

Questions 10-13.

DIRECTIONS: Select the letter preceding the word or phrase which completes each of the following statements correctly.

10. The library's title card for the book THE LATE GEORGE APLEY can be found by looking in the card catalog under   10._____

    A. Apley, George   B. The   C. Late   D. George   E. Apley

11. A catalog card for a book by John F. Kennedy would be found in the drawer labelled   11._____

    A. JEFFERSON-JOHNSON,ROY
    B. PRESCOTT-PRICELESS
    C. KIERNAN-KLAY
    D. U.S.PRESIDENT-U.S.SOCIAL SECURITY
    E. KENNEBEC-KIERKEGAARD

12. The title cards for these three periodicals would be found in the card catalog arranged in which of the following orders: 12._____

    A. NEW YORKER, NEWSWEEK, NEW YORK TIMES MAGAZINE
    B. NEWSWEEK, NEW YORKER, NEW YORK TIMES MAGAZINE
    C. NEW YORK TIMES MAGAZINE, NEW YORKER, NEWSWEEK
    D. NEW YORKER, NEW YORK TIMES MAGAZINE, NEWSWEEK
    E. NEWSWEEK, NEW YORK TIMES MAGAZINE, NEW YORKER

13. A card for a copy of the U.N.Charter would be found in the catalog drawer marked   13._____

    A. TWENTIETH-UNAMUNO
    B. UNITED MINE WORKERS-UNITED SHOE MACHINERY
    C. U.S.BUREAU-U.S. CONGRESS
    D. U.S.SOCIAL POLICY-UNIVERSITAS
    E. CHANCEL-CIARDI

II. UNDERSTANDING ENTRIES IN A PERIODICAL INDEX

Questions 14-25.

DIRECTIONS: The following items are excerpts from THE READERS' GUIDE TO PERIODICAL LITERATURE. Identify each lettered section of the entries by placing the correct letters in the spaces.(There are more letters than spaces, so some of the letters will not be used.)

```
A ─── UNITED NATIONS                V
         Ambassador Goldberg holds news conference at        H ─── Security Council
         New York; transcript of conference,                      Security Council urged to respond to
B ───    July 28, 1965; with questions and answers.  ─── U    challenge in southeast Asia; letter,
         A. J. Goldberg. Dept. State Bul 53:272+         M ─── July 30, 1965. A. J. Goldberg. Dept
C ───    Ag 16 '65                              ─── T         State Bul  53:278-80+  Ag 16, '65
         U.N. out of its teens. I.D. Talmadge. il Sr Schol ─── S    L   •I   J   K
E ───    87:16-17+  S 16 '65
D ───    Whatever became of the United Nations?  ─── Q
         America 113:235  S 4 '65
         F    R
                        Charter ──────────── P
         Up-dating the pre-atomic United Nations; address,
         June 20, 1965. C.P. Romulo. Vital Speeches
         31:658-61 Ag 15 '65; Excerpts. Sat R 48:34-5+   ─── O
         Jl 24 '65 ──────── N
                        G
```

14. Title of magazine containing a transcript of a news con-conference held by U.N. Ambassador Arthur Goldberg.   14.____

15. Magazine in which the full text of C.P. Romulo's address on the U.N. appears.   15.____

16. Author of an article titled U.N. OUT OF ITS TEENS.   16.____

17. Date on which Ambassador Goldberg wrote a letter urging the Security Council to respond to the challenge of southeast Asia.   17.____

18. Title of an article for which no author is listed.   18.____

19. Date of the SATURDAY REVIEW issue which contains excerpts of a speech called "Up-Dating the Pre-Atomic United Nations."   19.____

20. Pages in the DEPARTMENT OF STATE BULLETIN on which Ambassador Goldberg's letter appears.   20.____

21. Symbol indicating that the letter is continued on a later page.   21.____

22. Volume number of the magazine in which the article by I.D. Talmadge is printed.   22.____

23. Symbols meaning September 16, 1965.   23.____

24. The general subject heading under which all five articles are listed.   24.____

25. A subject heading subdivision.   25.____

Questions 26-27.

    DIRECTIONS: Select the letter preceding the phrase which completes each of the following statements correctly.

26. To determine whether or not the library has THE MAGAZINE OF AMERICAN HISTORY, check in   26.____

    A. the list of magazine titles in the front of THE READERS' GUIDE TO PERIODICAL LITERATURE
    B. the library's card catalog

C. Ulrich's GUIDE TO PERIODICALS
D. SATURDAY REVIEW
E. THE LIBRARY JOURNAL

27. THE READERS' GUIDE is a good place to look for material on the Job Corps because it 27._____

    A. indexes only the best books and magazines in each field
    B. is a guide to articles on many subjects appearing in all of the library's periodicals
    C. indexes recent discussions on the subject in many magazines
    D. specializes in official government information
    E. does all of the above

III. IDENTIFYING LIBRARY TERMS

Questions 28-32.

DIRECTIONS: Match the correct definitions with these terms by placing the correct letters in the blanks. (Some of the letters will not be used.)

28. Bibliography   A. Word or phrase printed in A. Word or phrase printed in log to indicate the major log to indicate the major   28._____

29. Anthology   B. Brief written summary of the major ideas presented in an article or book   29._____

30. Index   C. List of books and/or articles on one subject or by one author   30._____

31. Abstract   D. Collection of selections from the writings of one or several authors   31._____

32. Subject heading   E. Written account of a person's life   32._____

                         F. Alphabetical list of subjects with the pages on which they are to be found in a book or periodical

                         G. Subordinate, usually explanatory title, additional to the main title and usually printed below it

IV. FINDING A BOOK BY ITS CALL NUMBER

Questions 33-38.

DIRECTIONS: The Library of Congress classification system call numbers shown below are arranged in order, just as the books bearing those call numbers would be arranged on the shelves. To show where other call numbers would be located, select the letter of the CORRECT ANSWER.

A.	B.	C.	D.	E.	F.	G.	H.	I.	J.	K.
PS 201 .L67 1961	PS 201 .M44	PS 208 .B87 1944	PS 351 .D7	PS 351 .D77	PS 3513 .A2	PS 3515 .D72	PS 3515.3 A66	PS 3526 .N21	PS 3526.17 P2	PS 3526.37 A10

L.	M.	N.
PS 3526.37 C20	PS 3526.37 C37	PT 1 .R2

33. A book with the call number PS 201 .L67 would be shelved

   A. Before A B. Between A & B C. Between B & C
   D. Between C & D E. Between D & E

34. A book with the call number PS 208 .B87 1944a would be shelved

   A. Between A & B B. Between C & D C. Between B & C
   D. Between C & D E. Between D & E

35. A book with the call number PS 351 D8 would be shelved

   A. Between C & D B. Between D & E C. Between E & F
   D. Between F & G E. Between G & H

36. A book with the call number PS 3526.3 M53 would be shelved

   A. Between L & M B. Between J & K C. Between K & L
   D. Between M & O E. Between O & P

37. A book with the call number PS 3526.37 C205 would be shelved

   A. Between L & M B. Between N & O C. Between M & N
   D. Between O & P E. Between P & Q

38. A book with the call number PS 3526.37 C3 would be shelved

   A. Between M & N B. Between L & M C. Between N & O
   D. Between O & P E. Between P & Q

V. General

Questions 39-40.

DIRECTIONS: Each question or incomplete statement is followed by several suggested answers or completions. Select the one that BEST answers the question or completes the statement. *PRINT THE LETTER OF THE CORRECT ANSWER IN TEE SPACE AT THE RIGHT.*

39. When it is finished (in 610 volumes), the _____ will be the MOST monumental national bibliography in the world.   39._____

    A. UNION LIST OF SERIALS IN LIBRARIES OF THE UNITED STATES AND CAN-ADA
    B. UNITED STATES CATALOG
    C. READERS' GUIDE TO PERIODICAL LITERATURE
    D. NATIONAL UNION CATALOG

40. For those who wish to investigate the publishing companies and the people who control them, to locate the date a company was founded, who owned it, when it changed hands, what firm succeeded it, and other information of a similar nature, the periodical _____ is clearly invaluable.   40._____

    A. PUBLISHERS' TRADE LIST ANNUAL (PTLA)
    B. CUMULATIVE BOOK INDEX
    C. AMERICAN BOOKTRADE DIRECTORY
    D. PUBLISHERS WEEKLY

KEY (CORRECT ANSWERS)

1. I
2. B
3. E
4. C
5. D
6. G
7. H
8. J
9. A
10. C - The first word of the title which is not an article.
11. E - Every book in the library is listed in the card catalog under the author's name. (Warning: The "author" may be a society, a university, or some other institution.)
12. C - A title is alphabetized word-by-word; therefore, "New" comes before "Newsweek," "New York" before "New Yorker."
13. B - The United Nations, not an individual, is the author of this work.
14. T   16. Q   18. D   20. J   22. E   24. A   26. B   28. C   30. F   32. A
15. O   17. M   19. N   21. K   23. R   25. P/H   27. C   29. D   31. B
33. A - When two call numbers are identical except that one has a year or some other figure added at its end, the shorter call numbers comes first.
34. B
35. C - The numbers which follow a. are regarded as decimals; therefore, .D77 precedes .D8.
36. B - 3526.3 precedes 3526.37
37. A - .C20 precedes .C205
38. B - .C3 precedes .C37 (Read the call number line-by-line, and put a J before a P, before a PB, etc. Put a lower number before a greater one.)
39. D
40. D

www.ingramcontent.com/pod-product-compliance
Lightning Source LLC
Chambersburg PA
CBHW082148300426
44117CB00016B/2655